Boots COOKSHOP
CAKES
— AND CAKE —
DECORATING

Boots

COOKSHOP

CAKES
—AND CAKE—
DECORATING

Cover photograph by Chris Crofton
Inside photography by Fred Mancini

Published on behalf of
The Boots Company plc, Nottingham
by Hamlyn Publishing,
a division of The Hamlyn Publishing Group Ltd,
Bridge House, London Road, Twickenham, Middlesex, England

ISBN 0 600 32552 0

First published under the title
*Hamlyn All Colour Book of
Cakes and Cake Decorating*

Set in Gill Sans
by Photocomp Ltd, Birmingham

Printed in Italy

Contents

Useful Facts & Figures

Notes on metrication

In this book quantities are given in metric and Imperial measures. Exact conversion from Imperial to metric does not usually give very convenient working quantities and so the metric measures have been rounded off into units of 25 grams. The table below shows the recommended equivalents.

Ounces	Approx g to nearest whole figure	Recommended conversion to nearest unit of 25
1	28	25
2	57	50
3	85	75
4	113	100
5	142	150
6	170	175
7	198	200
8	227	225
9	255	250
10	283	275
11	312	300
12	340	350
13	368	375
14	396	400
15	425	425
16 (1 lb)	454	450
17	482	475
18	510	500
19	539	550
20 (1¼ lb)	567	575

Note: When converting quantities over 20 oz first add the appropriate figures in the centre column, then adjust to the nearest unit of 25. As a general guide, 1 kg (1000 g) equals 2·2 lb or about 2 lb 3 oz. This method of conversion gives good results in nearly all cases, although in certain pastry and cake recipes a more accurate conversion is necessary to produce a balanced recipe.

Liquid measures

The millilitre has been used in this book and the following table gives a few examples.

Imperial	Approx ml to nearest whole figure	Recommended ml
¼ pint	142	150 ml
½ pint	283	300 ml
¾ pint	425	450 ml
1 pint	567	600 ml
1½ pints	851	900 ml
1¾ pints	992	1000 ml (1 litre)

Spoon measures All spoon measures given in this book are level unless otherwise stated.

Can sizes At present, cans are marked with the exact (usually to the nearest whole number) metric equivalent of the Imperial weight of the contents, so we have followed this practice when giving can sizes.

Oven temperatures

The table below gives recommended equivalents.

	°C	°F	Gas
Very cool	110	225	¼
	120	250	½
Cool	140	275	1
	150	300	2
Moderate	160	325	3
	180	350	4
Moderately hot	190	375	5
	200	400	6
Hot	220	425	7
	230	450	8
Very hot	240	475	9

Note: *When making any of the recipes in this book, only follow one set of measures as they are not interchangeable.*

Introduction

Cake Making Equipment

There is a vast selection of equipment available on the market, varying in shape, size and type of finish. The price range is as broad as the choice and is usually significant of the quality. It is not necessary to own a wide variety, a small selection of basic tins is quite adequate for most baking purposes. This should include a pair of sandwich tins, a deep cake tin, a loaf tin and a Swiss roll tin. The type of finish chosen when buying tins should be considered in terms of the price, the quality desired and the expected usage of the tins. For instance, tins that are likely to be used frequently need to be of better quality than a tin which may only be used on certain occasions. It is worth remembering that good-quality tins, well looked after, will last a long time.

There are many types of non-stick finishes and coatings available, some of which are very effective. However, some of the inexpensive non-stick tins may be disappointing if they are to receive heavy use. There are many different shapes of tins including round, deep cake tins, sandwich tins, square and oblong cake tins, loaf tins, Swiss roll tins and some unusual decorative tins. Loose-bottomed tins, both round and square, are useful when baking large or delicate cakes. Springform tins are round tins which have loose bottoms and sides. The side has a clip attached to a spring which, when released, frees the base from its groove. Adjustable loaf tins are slightly unusual. Each section of these tins is clipped together and may be extended to give a larger tin. Removal of cakes from these tins is easy due to the fact that the sides drop away leaving the cake on the base.

It is most important that cake tins are well treated, to ensure that they are effective and have a long life. The manufacturer's instructions for use, cleaning and storage should always be strictly followed, however, there are a few general points to remember. Most tins should be well greased before use and should also be washed or soaked immediately after use. Abrasive cleaning powders and pads should be avoided. Sharp or pointed knives should never be used to remove cakes from their tins or to cut anything in the tin. Metal objects should generally not be used with non-stick tins except with extreme care. Tins should be stored in a dry, ventilated cupboard where they will not rust. Non-stick tins should not be stacked together without some form of wrapping or interleaving to prevent scratching.

A recipe may call for the tin to be lined or coated with flour. A lightly greased tin may be coated with flour by sprinkling a little flour into it and tapping gently whilst tilting the tin to spread the flour evenly. Any excess flour should be tipped out. Other linings include greaseproof paper, non-stick baking parchment and rice paper. The lining used should fit the tin smoothly and exactly. If the tin is to be bottom-lined, the outline of the base should be drawn on the paper, cut out and placed in the tin.

To Line a Straight-Sided Round or Square Tin.

Draw around the base of the tin on greaseproof paper and cut out a circle slightly smaller than the tin. Cut a strip of greaseproof paper long enough to go around the inside of the tin and approximately 5 cm/2 in deeper than the tin. Make a 2·5-cm/1-in fold along the length of the strip and snip it all along at intervals of approximately 1 cm/½ in. The greaseproof paper will adhere to the sides of the tin if they are lightly greased. Place the strip around the inside of the tin, overlapping the slits in the base. Grease the sides well then place the circle of greaseproof paper in the base and grease well. The paper should sit slightly above the side of the tin.

To Line a Swiss Roll or Loaf Tin.

Place the tin on a sheet of greaseproof paper allowing enough paper on each side to come up the sides of the tin and overlap slightly at the top. Draw around the shape of the tin and cut out an oblong of paper allowing for the depth of the sides. Cut inwards from each corner to the corner point on the outline of the tin. Lower the paper into the base of the lightly greased tin with the bottom of each slit in the base of each corner. Neatly fold and overlap the cut greaseproof paper inside each corner, greasing the piece lying underneath slightly in order to hold both pieces flat. Grease the paper well before placing the mixture in the tin.

All the tins in this book have been identified in terms of their dimensions apart from loaf tins. In this case we have used either a 450-g/1-lb or 1-kg/2-lb tin.

Cake Making Methods

The basic ingredients that go into making a cake are fat, flour, sugar and eggs. The texture of the cake is governed by the method of preparation and the proportions of ingredients.

The methods of cake making have been revolutionised over the years although we still retain some of the traditional methods. With the introduction of the soft margarines came the all-in-one method of cake making. All the ingredients are put into a bowl and beaten together until smooth. As there is no creaming involved to incorporate air, which in turn makes the cake rise, an extra raising agent is required when using this method.

The creaming method is probably the most well-known and widely-used method. The fat and sugar are beaten together until pale and fluffy in texture, before the other ingredients are added.

The rubbing-in method is used for making less rich cakes and some biscuit mixtures.

The melting method is very easy and is used in the making of gingerbreads, brandy snaps etc. The fat, syrup and sugar are melted over a low heat, before adding the other ingredients.

The whisking method is used for fatless sponges, Swiss rolls and Genoese-type cakes. The sugar and eggs are whisked in a basin over hot water until really thick and creamy.

Helpful Hints
Positions of cakes in the oven. Unless otherwise stated, cakes should aways be cooked in the centre of the oven. If there is not a true centre shelf, use a slightly lower, rather than a higher,

shelf. If you are cooking two cakes at once, place them underneath each other rather than on the same shelf, and change positions halfway through cooking.

Temperature of ingredients: all ingredients should be at room temperature before use to ensure a successful cake.

Ovens: always preheat the oven for at least 15 minutes before using. Individual ovens vary in temperature, so it is important to know your oven, especially where cakes are concerned.

Measuring spoons: all spoon measurements refer to the British Standard measuring spoons, which are plastic and can be purchased in any good department store.

Fruit: dried fruit is normally purchased ready for use, but if it is not, wash and rub in a tea-towel. Leave in a warm place until completely dry.

Eggs: the EEC regulations now stipulate that eggs must be graded according to their weight and numbered accordingly. We have used a size 3 egg throughout all the recipes unless otherwise stipulated. It is important to use the correct size of egg with the metric measurements, as cake recipes are particularly critical.

Testing a cake: the most reliable way of testing a cake to see if it is cooked is to insert a metal skewer into the middle of the cake. If it comes out clean, the cake is ready. Another method is to gently press the centre of the cake. If it is firm and beginning to shrink away from the sides of the tin, then it is cooked.

Freezing: all cakes and biscuits freeze well. Cakes can be frozen either iced or un-iced depending upon the type of icing. Butter and fudge icing freeze well, but glacé icing, frosting and royal icing are not to be recommended. It is not necessary to freeze rich fruit cakes as they improve with keeping for up to 6 months.

If freezing a layered cake, wrap each layer with a sheet of greaseproof paper and pack in a polythene bag or rigid container.

If freezing an iced cake, open-freeze on a baking sheet until firm, then pack in a rigid container.

Gâteaux and novelty cakes are particularly suitable for this method of freezing, but it is advisable to put the final decorations on when the cake has thawed.

Icing Equipment

The phrase, the right tool for the right job, is very relevant where applied to the art of icing. Using the correct piece of equipment not only makes icing easy but also fun! There is a fantastic range of equipment on the market to choose from, but to begin with, one only needs the basics.

Piping bags: these can be purchased or handmade. When purchased the bags are usually nylon or plastic and are generally fairly large. Basically, they are designed to accommodate the larger nozzles, although some have a special screw attachment which permits the use of small nozzles. Handmade greaseproof paper bags are suitable for royal icing as they are easier to control for fine work (see page 72 for making a handmade bag.)

Piping nozzles: these are made in both metal and plastic. The metal ones are generally better as they give more definition. Always buy good-quality nozzles, checking that the tip of the nozzle is a perfect shape and free from any dents. The seam where the metal has been joined should be smooth to the touch. The larger nozzles are suitable for piping butter icings, meringues, choux pastry, cream etc. The small nozzles are used for piping more intricate work on wedding cakes, for example. Some tubes have a thread enabling them to be used in conjunction with the screw attachments.

Cake boards: these can be bought in a variety of sizes and thicknesses and come in either silver or gold. They are ideal for large celebration and novelty cakes.

Turntables: these are by no means essential but an absolute boon to those who do a lot of royal iced cakes. If you do not want to go to the expense of purchasing a turntable, place the board containing the cake on an upturned plate. To make it a little easier to pipe around the bottom edge, stand the plate on a large upturned bowl, ensuring it is stable.

Straight edge: this is a smooth rule without any markings used to flat ice cakes.

Plastic scrapers: these are used to smooth the sides of cakes. They can be bought either plain or with a serrated edge.

Palette knife: this is an invaluable flat-bladed, pliable knife used for applying icing and making attractive designs.

Greaseproof, waxed and parchment paper: these are used for runouts, lining tins, piping bags, and chocolate shapes.

Traditional Favourites

Here you will find a selection of well-known traditional recipes such as Dundee cake and Battenburg together with some less usual ones. Many of these are good freezer candidates, enabling you to bake them at your leisure and always have a goody to offer unexpected guests. The rich fruit cake chart will be invaluable for making those special occasion cakes in a range of sizes.

BATTENBURG

175 g/6 oz butter or margarine
175 g/6 oz caster sugar
3 eggs
175 g/6 oz self-raising flour
1 tablespoon cocoa powder
1 tablespoon hot water
grated rind of 1 lemon
Decoration:
lemon curd
450 g/1 lb almond paste
(page 70)
caster sugar

Make the cake as for the Basic Victoria Sandwich (opposite). Divide the mixture in half. To one half add the cocoa powder blended in hot water and to the other add the lemon rind. Line and grease an 18-cm/7-in square cake tin and divide down the centre with a strip of folded greaseproof paper. Place the chocolate mixture in one side and the lemon in the other. Bake in a moderate oven (160C, 325F, gas 3) for 40-50 minutes. Turn out and cool on a wire tray.

Trim the edges of the cake and cut each half in two, lengthways, making four strips. Join alternate colours together in two layers, sandwiching with lemon curd. Roll the almond paste into an oblong 20 x 37 cm/8 x 15 in. Spread the outside of the assembled cake with lemon curd and place in the centre of the almond paste. Carefully ease the almond paste around the cake with the join underneath. Trim and finish as shown in the picture.

BASIC VICTORIA SANDWICH

100 g/4 oz butter or margarine
100 g/4 oz caster sugar
2 eggs
100 g/4 oz self-raising flour
Filling and Decoration:
3-4 tablespoons raspberry jam
icing sugar

Cream the butter and sugar together until light and fluffy. Beat in the eggs one at a time, adding a little of the flour with the second egg. Fold in the remaining flour using a metal spoon. Place the mixture in a bottom-lined and greased 20-cm/8-in sandwich tin or in two 18-cm/7-in sandwich tins. Bake in a moderate oven (160C, 325F, gas 3), 35-40 minutes for the 20-cm/8-in cake and 25-35 minutes for the 18-cm/7-in cakes. Turn out and cool on a wire tray.

To assemble the cake, first split the larger cake. Sandwich the cakes or two halves with the raspberry jam. Lay a doily on top of the cake and sprinkle with icing sugar. Carefully lift off the doily to leave a design on the surface of the cake.

Basic Victoria Sandwich and Battenburg

Strawberry Gâteau

Basic Genoese sponge:
50 g/2 oz butter or margarine
75 g/3 oz caster sugar
3 eggs
75 g/3 oz plain flour
Filling and Decoration:
300 ml/½ pint double cream
225 g/8 oz strawberries
icing sugar

To make the basic Genoese sponge, melt the butter and allow to cool. Put the sugar and eggs into a large mixing bowl and place over a saucepan of hot water. Whisk until the mixture is thick and pale in colour and forms a trail when the whisk is lifted. Sieve the flour twice and fold into the whisked mixture together with the melted butter. Place in two bottom-lined and greased 18-cm/7-in sandwich tins. Bake in a moderately hot oven (190 C, 375 F, gas 5) for 20-25 minutes. Turn out carefully and cool on a wire tray.

To fill and decorate the cake, lightly whip the cream and slice the strawberries, mix together one-third of the cream with some of the sliced fruit and use to spread over one of the cakes. Place the second cake on top. Spread some of the remaining cream over the top. Place the rest in a piping bag fitted with a star nozzle and pipe swirls around the top edge. Decorate with the remaining strawberries.

Swiss Roll

50 g/2 oz caster sugar
2 eggs
50 g/2 oz plain flour
caster sugar
Filling and Icing:
3-4 tablespoons lemon curd
225 g/8 oz lemon butter icing
(page 68)
chocolate shapes (page 73)

Place the sugar and eggs in a mixing bowl and whisk over a saucepan of hot water until the mixture is thick and pale in colour and forms a trail when lifted. Sieve the flour twice and fold into the mixture. Place the mixture in a lined and greased 28 x 18-cm/11 x 7-in Swiss roll tin, smoothing over evenly. Bake in a moderately hot oven (200 C, 400 F, gas 6) for 8-10 minutes.

Meanwhile, place a damp tea-towel on a working surface and lay a sheet of greaseproof paper on top.

Sprinkle very lightly with caster sugar. Immediately the Swiss roll is cooked turn out on to the sugared paper. Remove the lining paper and trim the crusty edges. Make an indentation with a knife along the shortest edge nearest to you. Lay a sheet of clean greaseproof paper on top of the Swiss roll, then roll up tightly. Allow to cool.

To fill and decorate, carefully unroll the Swiss roll.. Remove the greaseproof paper, spread with the lemon curd and re-roll. Make the butter icing and place in a piping bag fitted with a star nozzle. Pipe rows of icing along the roll and decorate with chocolate shapes.

Dundee Cake

225 g/8 oz butter or margarine
225 g/8 oz caster sugar
grated rind of 1 orange
5 eggs
300 g/11 oz plain flour
½ teaspoon baking powder
1 teaspoon ground mixed spice
pinch of grated nutmeg
225 g/8 oz currants
225 g/8 oz sultanas
225 g/8 oz raisins
50 g/2 oz glacé cherries, chopped
100 g/4 oz chopped mixed peel
Decoration:
50 g/2 oz whole blanched almonds

Place all the ingredients in a mixing bowl and beat with a wooden spoon until well mixed. Place in a lined and greased 20-cm/8-in cake tin and smooth the top with the back of a hot, wet metal spoon. Arrange the whole almonds in circles over the top. Bake in a cool oven (150 C, 300 F, gas 2) for 3½-4 hours. Leave to cool in the tin for five minutes, then turn out and finish cooling on a wire tray.

Note: Unblanched almonds are normally a little less expensive to purchase. To blanch them, place in a small bowl and pour on some boiling water. Leave for 2-3 minutes then take out one at a time and peel off the skins, which will come away easily.

Strawberry Gâteau and Swiss Roll

RICH FRUIT CAKE

| | 18 cm/7 in | 20 cm/8 in | 23 cm/9 in | 25 cm/10 in | 28 cm/11 in |
	15 cm/6 in	18 cm/7 in	20 cm/8 in	23 cm/9 in	25 cm/10in
Butter	100 g/4 oz	150 g/5 oz	200 g/7 oz	250 g/9 oz	300 g/11 oz
Dark soft brown sugar	150 g/5 oz	175 g/6 oz	225 g/8 oz	275 g/10 oz	350 g/12 oz
Black treacle	1 tablespoon	1 tablespoon	1 tablespoon	1 tablespoon	1½ tablespoons
Eggs	3	4	5	6	7
Plain flour	175 g/6 oz	200 g/7 oz	250 g/9 oz	300 g/11 oz	400 g/14 oz
Ground mixed spice	¾ teaspoon	1 teaspoon	1¼ teaspoons	1½ teaspoons	1½ teaspoons
Grated nutmeg	¼ teaspoon	½ teaspoon	½ teaspoon	¾ teaspoon	¾ teaspoon
Ground almonds	40 g/1½ oz	50 g/2 oz	65 g/2½ oz	75 g/3 oz	90 g/3½ oz
Grated lemon rind	1 lemon	1 lemon	1 lemon	2 lemons	2 lemons
Grated orange rind	1 orange	1 orange	1 orange	2 oranges	2 oranges
Chopped almonds	50 g/2 oz	65 g/2½ oz	90 3½ oz	125 g/4 oz	150 g/5 oz
Glacé cherries	50 g/2 oz	65 g/2½ oz	90 g/3½ oz	125 g/4 oz	150 g/5 oz
Raisins	75 g/3 oz	100 g/4 oz	150 g/5 oz	175 g/6 oz	200 g/7 oz
Sultanas	150 g/5 oz	200 g/7 oz	250 g/9 oz	300 g/11 oz	375 g/13 oz
Currants	225 g/8 oz	275 g/10 oz	375 g/13 oz	450 g/1 lb	575 g/1¼ lb
Chopped mixed peel	50 g/2 oz	65 g/2½ oz	90 g/3½ oz	125 g/4 oz	150 g/5 oz
Brandy	1 tablespoon	2 tablespoons	2 tablespoons	3 tablespoons	3 tablespoons
Orange juice	1 tablespoon	1 tablespoon	2 tablespoons	2 tablespoons	3 tablespoons

This rich fruit cake is suitable for all types of special occasions, such as weddings, christenings, Christmas and birthdays.

To keep the cake moist and to give it a good flavour, prick the base of the cooked, upturned cake with a skewer and pour over a little brandy. Stand on a wire tray for a few hours to allow the brandy to penetrate. Wrap the cake well and store in an airtight tin. It will keep for up to 6 months.

To make the fruit cake, cream the butter and sugar together until light and fluffy. Beat in the black treacle. Add the eggs one at a time, adding a little of the flour with each egg after the first. Mix the flour with all the remaining ingredients except the brandy and orange juice, and gradually fold into the creamed mixture. Stir in the brandy and orange juice. Place the mixture in a tin lined with double greaseproof paper and greased. Smooth the top of the cake using the back of a hot, wet metal spoon. Protect the outside of the tin with newspaper and bake in a cool oven (140C, 275F, gas 1). Check the cake after the first 3 hours, then at intervals after that. The smallest of the cakes should be checked after the first 2½ hours. (To test the cake, see pages 12 and 13.) Allow the cake to cool in the tin for 15 minutes before removing and cool completely on a wire tray.

CRYSTALLISED FRUIT CAKE

175 g/6 oz butter or margarine
175 g/6 oz soft brown sugar
3 eggs
225 g/8 oz plain flour
1 teaspoon ground mixed spice
grated rind of 1 orange
225 g/8 oz raisins
50 g/2 oz stem ginger, chopped
50 g/2 oz blanched almonds, chopped
50 g/2 oz angelica, chopped
50 g/2 oz glacé cherries, chopped
50 g/2 oz brazil nuts, chopped
1-2 tablespoons orange juice
Decoration:
crystallised ginger, whole almonds, brazil nuts and
glacé cherries
sieved apricot jam

Cream the butter and sugar together until lightly fluffy. Beat in the eggs one at a time, adding a little of the sieved flour with each egg after the first. Fold in the remaining flour and spice with the orange rind, raisins, ginger, blanched almonds, angelica, cherries, brazil nuts

Dundee Cake (page 18)

and sufficient orange juice to give a soft dropping consistency.

Place in a lined and greased 18-cm/7-in cake tin. Smooth the top with the back of a hot, wet metal spoon. Arrange rows of ginger, almonds, brazil nuts, and cherries on top of the cake. Bake in a cool oven (140 C, 275 F, gas 1) for 2½-3 hours. Allow to cool slightly before removing from the tin and placing on a wire tray. Glaze with warmed apricot jam while the cake is still warm.

FRUIT 'N' NUT CAKE

150 g/5 oz butter or margarine
6 tablespoons golden syrup
100 g/4 oz dried apricots
50 g/2 oz sultanas
225 g/8 oz raisins
100 g/4 oz currants
50 g/2 oz almonds, chopped
10 tablespoons milk
225 g/8 oz plain flour
pinch of grated nutmeg
grated rind of 1 orange
2 eggs
½ teaspoon bicarbonate of soda
Topping:
50 g/2 oz dried apricots, chopped
50 g/2 oz whole almonds
25 g/1 oz glacé cherries
2 tablespoons honey

Place the butter, syrup, fruit, nuts and milk in a saucepan and melt over a low heat. Simmer gently for 5 minutes. Cool slightly. Place the flour, nutmeg and orange rind in a bowl and add the eggs. Stir the bicarbonate of soda into the cooked fruit mixture and add to the dry ingredients. Mix well and place in a lined and greased 18-cm/7-in square cake tin. Smooth the surface and bake in a cool oven (150 C, 300 F, gas 2) for 1¾-2 hours. Turn out and cool on a wire tray.

To make the topping. Place all the ingredients in a saucepan and heat until thoroughly mixed. Spread on top of the cake.

GINGERBREAD RING CAKE

100 g/4 oz butter or margarine
100 g/4 oz soft brown sugar
175 g/6 oz black treacle
225 g/8 oz plain flour
3-4 teaspoons ground ginger
½ teaspoon ground cinnamon
1 egg, beaten
½ teaspoon bicarbonate of soda
6 tablespoons milk
Icing and Decoration:
100 g/4 oz glacé icing (see page 68)
crystallised ginger

Melt the butter, sugar and treacle over a low heat until dissolved. Sieve the flour and spices into a bowl and pour in the melted mixture and egg. Dissolve the bicarbonate of soda in the milk and stir into the flour mixture, mixing well. Pour quickly into a greased and floured 20-cm/8-in ring tin. Bake in a moderate oven (160 C, 325 F, gas 3) for 1-1¼ hours. Leave in the tin for a few minutes before turning out to cool on a wire tray.

To ice and decorate the cake make the glacé icing and pour over the cake allowing it to run down the sides. Decorate with crystallised ginger.

Variations
Fruity gingerbread Add 75 g/3 oz raisins with the dry ingredients.
Orange gingerbread Add the coarsely grated rind of 2 oranges with the dry ingredients.
Nutty gingerbread Add 100 g/4 oz chopped walnuts with the dry ingredients.

Madeira Cake (opposite)

Cherry Madeira Cake

MADEIRA CAKE

175 g/6 oz butter
175 g/6 oz caster sugar
grated rind of 1 lemon
3 eggs
225 g/8 oz plain flour
1 ½ teaspoons baking powder
2 tablespoons warm water
piece of candied peel

Cream the butter and sugar together until light and fluffy. Beat in the lemon rind. Beat in the eggs one at a time, adding a little of the flour with each egg after the first. Fold in the remaining flour and baking powder using a metal spoon. Gently fold in the water to give a soft dropping consistency. Place in a bottom-lined and greased 18-cm/7-in cake tin. Place the candied peel on the centre of the cake. Bake in a moderate oven (160 C, 325 F, gas 3) for 1 ¼-1 ½ hours. Allow to cool slightly in the tin before turning out and cooling on a wire tray.

CHERRY MADEIRA CAKE

175 g/6 oz butter or margarine
175 g/6 oz caster sugar
3 eggs
225 g/8 oz plain flour
½ teaspoon baking powder
175 g/6 oz glacé cherries, chopped
2 thin strips citron peel (optional)

Cream the butter and sugar together until light and fluffy. Beat in the eggs one at a time, adding a little of the flour with each egg after the first. Fold in the rest of the flour with the baking powder and cherries. Place in a lined and greased 1-kg/2-lb loaf tin, and arrange the peel over the centre. Bake in a moderate oven (160 C, 325 F, gas 3) for 1 ¼-1 ½ hours. Turn out and cool on a wire tray.

Variations
Ginger cake Add 2 teaspoons ground ginger and 50 g/2 oz chopped crystallised ginger to the mixture.
Coconut and lemon cake Add 50 g/2 oz desiccated coconut, the grated rind of 1 lemon and 2 tablespoons milk to the mixture.

CHOCOLATE AND ALMOND CAKE

175 g/6 oz butter or margarine
175 g/6 oz caster sugar
100 g/4 oz plain chocolate, melted
50 g/2 oz ground almonds
4 eggs, separated
50 g/2 oz self-raising flour
25 g/1 oz cornflour
Icing and Decoration:
225 g/8 oz chocolate butter icing
(page 68)
50 g/2 oz chopped almonds, toasted
few whole almonds, dipped
in melted chocolate
few mimosa balls

Cream the butter and sugar together until light and fluffy. Beat in the melted chocolate, ground almonds and egg yolks. Fold in the flour and cornflour. Whisk the egg whites until stiff, then carefully fold into the cake mixture. Divide the mixture between two bottom-lined and greased 20-cm/8-in sandwich tins. Bake in a moderate oven (160 C, 325 F, gas 3) for 40-45 minutes. Turn out and cool on a wire tray.

To ice and decorate the cake, make the icing and use two thirds to sandwich the cakes together and cover the sides. Roll the sides in the toasted almonds. Smooth the remaining icing over the surface and decorate with whole almonds half dipped in melted chocolate. Arrange the almonds to form flowers with a mimosa ball in the centre.

ST CLEMENT'S RING CAKE

175 g/6 oz butter or margarine
175 g/6 oz caster sugar
3 eggs
100 g/4 oz self-raising flour
50 g/2 oz ground almonds
grated rind of 1 orange
grated rind of 1 lemon
Icing and Decoration:
225 g/8 oz lemon glacé icing
(page 68)
shredded orange and lemon rind

Cream the butter and sugar together until light and fluffy. Beat in the eggs one at a time, adding a little of the sieved flour with each egg after the first. Fold in the remaining flour with the ground almonds and fruit rinds. Place the mixture in a greased and floured 20-cm/8-in ring mould. Bake in a moderate oven (160 C, 325 F, gas 3) for 40-45 minutes. Turn out and cool on a wire tray.

To ice and decorate the cake, make the icing and pour over the cake allowing it to run down the sides. Decorate with shredded orange and lemon rind.

HAZELNUT COFFEE CAKE
(Illustrated on front cover)

100 g/4 oz butter or margarine
175 g/6 oz soft brown sugar
2 eggs
6 tablespoons milk
1 tablespoon coffee essence
75 g/3 oz hazelnuts, chopped
75 g/3 oz raisins
225 g/8 oz self-raising flour
1 teaspoon baking powder
Icing and Decoration:
225 g/8 oz coffee butter icing (page 68)
toasted hazelnuts

Place all the ingredients in a mixing bowl and beat with a wooden spoon until well mixed. Place in two bottom-lined and greased 20-cm/8-in sandwich tins. Bake in a moderate oven (160 C, 325 F, gas 3) for 30-40 minutes. Turn out and cool on a wire tray.

To ice and decorate the cake, make the icing following the recipe instructions. Sandwich the cakes together with a little of the icing, then spread the remainder over the top of the cake and pipe a border around the edge. Decorate with whole toasted hazelnuts.

St Clement's Ring Cake

Special Occasion Cakes

Occasions are always made that much more special when a beautiful cake is served. The following chapter gives recipes for many special cakes from a magnificent three-tier wedding cake to the more simple, yet imaginative Christmas cake.

THREE-TIER WEDDING CAKE

1 (30-cm/12-in) square rich fruit cake (page 20)
1 (23-cm/9-in) square rich fruit cake (page 20)
1 (15-cm/6-in) square rich fruit cake (page 20)
Icing and Decoration:
almond paste (page 70)
1 (35-cm/14-in) square silver cake board
1 (25-cm/10-in) square silver cake board
1 (10-cm/7-in) square silver cake board
royal icing (page 71)
primrose coloured piped roses (page 75)
small silver leaves
silver cake board edging
silver vase
8 cake pillars

Make the cakes, as directed, 2-3 months in advance so that they have time to mature.

To ice and decorate the cakes, cover the cakes with almond paste, as directed, 1-2 weeks before icing, and place the cakes on their appropriate cake boards.

Flat ice the cakes, as directed, until you have completed 4 or 5 layers of icing and have obtained a perfect flat surface. The thinner the layers of icing, the easier it will be to handle. Make primrose coloured roses, as directed, at least one day before using.

Cut out squares of greaseproof paper the actual size of the iced cakes and fold into quarters. Unfold and fold each edge into the centre to form 16 squares, making a crease along the folded edges. Place the unfolded greaseproof paper on top of each cake and using a pin, prick the four corners on each. Using a greaseproof piping bag fitted with a plain writing nozzle, pipe two straight lines of icing at right angles to each other. Repeat this design. This will then mark the positions for the pillars. Using a finer writing tube, pipe on top of these lines to give a more delicate effect.

To decorate the sides of the cake, cut a strip of greaseproof paper the size of one of the sides of each of the cakes and draw a scalloped edge along each, making five scallops on the large cake, four scallops on the middle-sized cake and three on the small cake. Place the paper against the sides of the cakes and prick these designs through using a pin. Using a plain writing nozzle, pipe small dots of icing along the scallops. Position a rose at the top of each scallop with a silver leaf at either side and secure with a little of the icing. Using the same writing nozzle, pipe a beading edge along the bottom edges of each cake. Then using a star-shaped nozzle, pipe a shell edge along the top edges. Arrange three roses in the corner of each cake and in the centre of the bottom two tiers.

Using a small palette knife, ice the silver boards with a thin layer of icing and allow to dry hard. Secure the silver paper edging to the boards with a little royal icing. Place the pillars in position and assemble the cakes at the last minute, placing the vase of flowers on top.

Three-Tier Wedding Cake

PINK CHRISTENING CAKE

*1 (20-cm/8-in) round rich
fruit cake (page 20)*
Icing and Decoration:
*almond paste (page 70)
1 (25-cm/10-in) round silver
cake board
royal icing (page 71)
pink food colouring*

Make the cake, as directed, 2-3 months in advance so that it has time to mature.

To ice and decorate the cake. Cover the cake with almond paste, as directed, 1-2 weeks before icing and place on the silver cake board. Make up the icing and reserve a little of the white icing for piping. Colour the remainder pink. Flat ice the cake as directed, using the pink icing. Using a small palette knife, cover the silver board with a thin layer of icing and allow to dry hard. Cut a strip of greaseproof paper the circumference and width of the sides of the cake and draw a scalloped edge, evenly all the way round. Place around the cake and secure with a pin and then prick through the design on to the cake. Remove the greaseproof paper and, using a greaseproof piping bag fitted with a writing nozzle, pipe small dots along the scallops with white icing, and vertical dots in between each scallop. Using the same nozzle, pipe the trellis along the bottom edge of the cake. Pipe a series of parallel lines at an angle all round the cake. Then pipe another layer of parallel lines over the top in the opposite direction. Repeat this twice, extending the length of the lines slightly over each layer. Pipe a line of small dots either side of the trellis. Using the same writing nozzle, pipe the name of the child to be christened. Pipe a row of stars, using a star-shaped nozzle along the top edge.

FONDANT-ICED CHRISTMAS CAKE

*1 (18-cm/7-in) round rich
fruit cake (page 20)*
Icing and Decoration:
*almond paste (page 70)
1 (20-cm/8-in) round silver
cake board
fondant icing (page 69)
red and green food colouring
candle
ribbon*

Make the cake, as directed, 2-3 months in advance so that it has time to mature.

To ice and decorate the cake, cover it with almond paste, as directed, 1-2 weeks before icing and place on a silver cake board. Make up the fondant icing as directed, reserving trimmings, and cover the cake. Allow to dry overnight before decorating. Using the trimmings of the fondant icing, colour a little green and some red and mould to resemble holly and berries. Arrange the holly in a circle on top of the cake and secure a candle in the centre. Tie a ribbon around the edge of the cake.

SNOW-PEAKED CAKE

*1 (15-cm/6-in) round rich
fruit cake (page 20)*
Icing and Decoration:
*almond paste (page 70)
1 (18-cm/7-in) round silver
cake board
royal icing (page 71)
Christmas cake decorations
ribbon*

Make the cake, as directed, 2-3 months in advance so that it has time to mature.

To ice and decorate the cake, cover the cake with almond paste, as directed, 1-2 weeks before icing and place on the silver cake board. Make up the icing, as directed, and flat ice the sides. When you have completed two or three layers of icing on the sides, rough ice the top. To rough ice, cover the top completely with icing and smooth evenly, then using the tip of a palette knife, dip it into the icing and press the tip of the knife onto the surface of the icing and draw away to form a peak. Repeat this process until the top of the cake is covered in peaks of icing. Decorate with Christmas decorations, and tie a ribbon around the cake.

CHRISTMAS TREE

1 (23 x 33-cm/9 x 13-in) sandwich
cake (boat cake page 57)
Icing and Decoration:
225 g/8 oz butter icing (page 68)
green food colouring
2 teaspoons cocoa powder
2 teaspoons boiling water
mint chocolate roll
candles
liquorice allsorts
small star
small piece ribbon

Cut out a piece of greaseproof paper to the same size as the cake. Draw the shape of the Christmas tree on the paper and use as a template to cut out the cake (see helpful hint). Cut out the tub for the tree from the spare pieces of cake.

To ice and decorate the cake, reserve one tablespoon of butter icing. Colour the remaining icing green and use to cover the cake completely. Fork the icing to give a branch effect. Cream the cocoa powder with the boiling water. Cool and mix with the remaining butter icing. Use the chocolate icing to cover the tub. Place the chocolate roll at the base of the tree as the trunk and put the tub in position. Decorate with candles, sweets, a star and a ribbon.

Helpful Hint. Cut a Christmas tree shape from paper and face it on the baked cake. Cut around the shape to make the tree. Left over pieces of cake may be frozen for future use or be incorporated in a trifle.

PARCEL CAKES

1 (23 x 33-cm/9 x 13-in) sandwich cake
(boat cake, page 57)
Icing and Decoration:
350 g/12 oz butter icing (page 68)
various food colourings
chocolate vermicelli
tinted dragees
silver balls

Cut the cake into small square or oblong shapes.

To ice and decorate the cakes, divide the butter icing into small portions and colour with various food colourings. Cover each square completely in butter icing and press chocolate vermicelli around some of the cakes using a palette knife. Using a greaseproof piping bag fitted with a ribbon nozzle, pipe the ribbons on the cakes. Decorate with tinted dragees or silver balls.

Variation

Instead of using butter icing to cover the cakes, they may be covered with thinly rolled out almond paste (see page 70). Brush the squares of cake with warmed apricot jam to make the almond paste stick. Decorate as liked with shapes moulded from almond paste.

Helpful Hint. To tint icings, dip a metal skewer into the bottle of food colouring and shake the drops from the skewer into the icing. This method ensures that the icing does not become too brightly coloured.

Christmas Tree and Parcel Cakes

MOTHER'S DAY CAKE

175 g/6 oz butter or margarine
175 g/6 oz caster sugar
3 eggs
100 g/4 oz glacé cherries
50 g/2 oz crystallised ginger, chopped
50 g/2 oz crystallised pineapple, chopped
50 g/2 oz citron peel, chopped
225 g/8 oz self-raising flour
Icing and Decoration:
225 g/8 oz glacé icing (page 68)
50 g/2 oz glacé cherries
2 tablespoons caster sugar
few pieces of angelica

Cream the butter with the sugar until pale and fluffy. Gradually, beat in the eggs. Wash, drain and chop the cherries. Add to the other chopped ingredients and coat thoroughly in 2 tablespoons of the measured flour. Sieve the flour over the creamed mixture and fold in evenly using a metal spoon. Gently fold in the chopped ingredients. Transfer the mixture to a lined and greased 20-cm/8-in cake tin, smooth over the surface and bake in a moderate oven (160 C, 325 F, gas 3) for 1¼ hours. Turn out and cool on a wire tray. Ice and decorate as shown in the picture.

SILVER WEDDING CAKE

1 (20-cm/8-in) square rich
fruit cake (page 20)
Icing and Decoration:
almond paste (page 70)
1 (23-cm/9-in) square cake
board in silver
royal icing (page 71)
crystallised flowers (page 74)
silver cake decorations (optional)
silver cake board edging

Make the cake, as directed, 2-3 months in advance so that it has time to mature.

To ice and decorate the cake. Cover the cake with almond paste, as directed, 1-2 weeks before icing and place on a silver cake board. Make up the icing and flat ice the cake, as directed. Decorate with crystallised flowers and silver cake decorations, if liked. Place the silver board edging around the sides of the cake, securing with a little icing. Pipe a shell border on the top and bottom edges of the cake.

SIMNEL CAKE

175 g/6 oz butter or margarine
175 g/6 oz dark soft brown sugar
3 eggs
225 g/8 oz self-raising flour
1 teaspoon mixed spice
350 g/12 oz sultanas
100 g/4 oz mixed chopped peel
225 g/8 oz raisins
50 g/2 oz almonds, chopped
4-5 tablespoons milk
Icing and Decorations:
675 g/1 ½ lb almond paste (page 70)
sieved apricot jam
little glacé icing (page 68)

Place all the cake ingredients in a mixing bowl and beat with a wooden spoon until well mixed. Place half the mixture in a prepared 20-cm/8-in cake tin. Roll out 225 g/8 oz of the almond paste into a circle measuring 20-cm/8-in. in diameter. Place the paste on top of the cake mixture and then spoon the remaining mixture over it, smoothing the surface evenly. Protect the outside of the tin with newspaper. Bake in a moderate oven (160 C, 325 F, gas 3) for 2 hours, then reduce the temperature to a cool oven (150 C, 300 F, gas 2) for a further 50-60 minutes. Allow to cool and turn out on to a wire tray.

To ice and decorate the cake, roll out 225 g/8 oz of the almond paste into a round to fit the top of the cake. Brush the top of the cake with apricot jam and secure the almond paste on top. Use a fork to separate the edge. Divide the remaining almond paste into 11 equal-sized pieces and roll into balls. Arrange them around the top edge of the cake, securing each with a little jam. Using a fork, press each ball firmly so that they flatten. Brush with a little beaten egg white and place under a hot grill until lightly browned. Pour the glacé icing into the centre.

Easter Chick (overleaf) and Simnel Cake

EASTER CHICK

1½ quantities Basic Victoria Sandwich
(page 16)
Icing and Decoration:
225 g/8 oz butter icing (page 68)
few drops of yellow food colouring
chocolate drops
50 g/2 oz almond paste, made-up
weight (page 70)*
red ribbon
Easter bonnet made from coloured
paper and fresh flowers (optional)

Make the cake mixture and divide it between a 300-ml/ ½-pint pudding basin and a 900-ml/1½-pint basin. Bake in a moderate oven (160C, 325F, gas 3) for 1 hour 20 minutes for the smaller cake and 1 hour 25 minutes for the larger one. Turn out and cool on a wire tray. Trim the smaller cake to make the head and stick it on top of the larger one with a little of the butter icing.

To ice and decorate the cakes, colour the butter icing with a yellow food colouring. Spread a little icing on top of the larger cake and place the smaller cake to form the neck of the chick. Cover the cakes completely with the icing and rough it up for a feather effect using a fork. Place chocolate drops on the cake to form eyes and shape a third of the almond paste to form a beak. Tie a bow around the neck and shape the remaining almond paste for the feet. Place an Easter bonnet with fresh flowers on top of the cake, if liked.
*If preferred, you can use ready-prepared almond paste available from most supermarkets.

GRANNY CAKE

175 g/6 oz butter or margarine
175 g/6 oz caster sugar
grated rind of 2 oranges
3 eggs
250 g/9 oz self-raising flour
1½ teaspooons baking powder
Filling and Icing:
50 g/2 oz butter
75 g/3 oz icing sugar, sieved
grated rind of 1 large orange
100 g/4 oz ground almonds
4 tablespoons orange juice
225 g/8 oz almond paste
(page 70)
2-3 tablespoons apricot jam,
warmed and sieved

350 g/12 oz fondant icing (page 69)
red and yellow food colouring
icing sugar
ribbon
moulded flowers and leaves
(page 75)

Place all the cake ingredients in a bowl and beat together, until smooth. Transfer the mixture to a bottom-lined and greased 20-cm/8-in cake tin. Bake in a moderate oven (180C, 350F, gas 4) for 1-1¼ hours.

To fill and ice the cake, cream the butter with the icing sugar and orange rind until pale and fluffy. Gradually, beat in the ground almonds and juice. Cut through the cake horizontally and sandwich the layers together with the butter cream. Cover the cake with almond paste as directed. Leave to dry out overnight.

Carefully colour the fondant icing by kneading in drops of the food colouring. Roll out on a surface sieved with icing sugar to give a round of approximately 36 cm/14 in. in diameter. Brush the cake with a little apricot jam. Carefully lift the fondant over the cake and smooth it down evenly, using fingertips dipped in sieved icing sugar or cornflour, and trim. Leave to dry, then finish as shown.

Granny Cake

VALENTINE'S CAKE

225 g/8 oz butter or margarine
225 g/8 oz caster sugar
grated rind of 2 lemons
4 eggs
225 g/8 oz self-raising flour
Icing and Decoration:
350 g/12 oz lemon butter icing
(page 68)
yellow food colouring
fresh flowers
angelica leaves
small pieces of fern (optional)

Cream the butter with the caster sugar and lemon rind until pale and fluffy. Gradually, beat in the eggs. Sieve the flour over the creamed mixture and fold in carefully using a metal spoon. Grease three heart-shaped tins measuring 23 cm/9 in, 18 cm/7 in and 12 cm/4¾ in from the point to the top of the heart. Divide the mixture proportionally between the three tins and bake in a moderate oven (160 C, 325 F, gas 3) for 30-40 minutes. Turn out and cool on a wire tray.

To ice and decorate the cakes, cover the top of each cake thinly with some of the butter icing. On a suitable cake board or plate, place all three cakes on top of each other with the larger cake on the bottom. Colour the remaining icing a delicate yellow and use some to cover the cake completely. Place the remaining butter icing in a greaseproof piping bag fitted with a small star-shaped nozzle and pipe an edging on the cake. Arrange fresh flowers on the cake together with angelica leaves and fern, if liked.

Helpful Hint. Heart-shaped silver cake boards are available, but if you have difficulty in obtaining one put the cake on a large round board. Alternatively, cut a large heart shape from thick cardboard and cover it with cooking foil.

Gâteaux

The mouth-watering gâteaux in this chapter may at first glance daunt you, but by following the clearly explained recipes and using the colour pictures as your guide, you will be able to achieve success and impress your family and guests. The helpful hints and drawings will guide you through the less easy stages. These gâteaux may be served as a dessert or be made for afternoon tea – the peach gâteaux makes a particularly delightful summer dessert.

HONEY HAZELNUT GÂTEAU

3 eggs
175 g/6 oz clear honey
100 g/4 oz hazelnuts, chopped
100 g/4 oz plain flour
Filling and Decoration:
450 ml/¾ pint double cream
4 tablespoons clear honey
100 g/4 oz hazelnuts, chopped
50 g/2 oz whole hazelnuts

Whisk the eggs with the honey until pale and thick. Meanwhile, lightly toast the chopped hazelnuts until pale golden in colour. Sieve the flour and mix with the hazelnuts then fold lightly into the whisked mixture. Turn into a lined and greased 23 × 33-cm/9 × 13-in Swiss roll tin and bake in a moderately hot oven (200 C, 400 F, gas 6) for 10-15 minutes. Turn out on to a wire tray, remove the greaseproof paper and leave to cool.

  Whip the cream with half the honey. Lightly toast the chopped hazelnuts. Cut the cake into three oblong pieces and sandwich together with half the cream. Spread the sides of the gâteau with cream and press the chopped hazelnuts onto them. Using a small star nozzle, pipe around the edge of the cake. Mix the whole hazelnuts with the remaining honey, warming it slightly if necessary, and carefully spoon over the top of the cake. Serve immediately.

MINTED LEMON GÂTEAU

100 g/4 oz caster sugar
3 eggs
75 g/3 oz plain flour
40 g/1 ½ oz butter or margarine, melted
few sprigs of mint, finely chopped
grated rind of 1 lemon
Decoration:
300 ml/½ pint of double cream
fresh lemon slices
few sprigs of crystallised mint (page 74)

Whisk the sugar and eggs together in a basin over a saucepan of hot water until the mixture is thick and pale in colour. Sieve the flour twice and fold into the whisked mixture with the melted butter, chopped mint and lemon rind. Place in a greased and floured 20-cm/8-in ring tin. Bake in a moderately hot oven (190 C, 375 F, gas 5) for 20 minutes. Turn out very carefully and cool on a wire tray.

  To decorate the gâteau, whip the cream and spread a little all over the gâteau. Pipe a border of cream around the top edge and decorate with halved fresh lemon slices and sprigs of crystallised mint.

Minted Lemon Gâteau and Honey Hazelnut Gâteau

AUSTRIAN COFFEE GÂTEAU

100 g/4 oz butter or margarine
100 g/4 oz caster sugar
2 eggs
100 g/4 oz self-raising flour
2 tablespoons coffee essence
grated rind of 1 lemon
Syrup:
150 ml/¼ pint black coffee
50 g/2 oz caster sugar
1 tablespoon brandy
Decoration:
300 ml/½ pint double cream
grated chocolate

Cream the butter and sugar together until light and fluffy. Add the eggs one at a time, adding a little of the flour with the second egg. Beat in the coffee essence, then fold in the remaining flour with the grated lemon rind. Place in a greased 20-cm/8-in ring tin and bake in a moderate oven (160 C, 325 F, gas 3) for 40-50 minutes. Turn out and cool on a wire tray.

To make the syrup, heat the coffee and sugar together in a saucepan until the sugar is dissolved, then add the brandy and simmer for 5 minutes. Allow to cool. Prick the cake with a skewer and pour over the syrup, a little at a time, until it is all absorbed.

To decorate the gâteau, whip the cream and spread a little over all of the cake. Using a nylon piping bag, pipe the remainder around the edge and decorate with the grated chocolate.

BLACK FOREST GÂTEAU

3 eggs
100 g/4 oz caster sugar
75 g/3 oz plain flour
15 g/½ oz cocoa powder
Filling:
1 (425 g/15-oz) can stoned black cherries
1 tablespoon arrowroot
Kirsch
300 ml/½ pint double cream
grated chocolate to decorate

Place the eggs and sugar in a basin and whisk over a saucepan of hot water until thick and pale in colour. Remove from the heat and continue to whisk until cool.

Black Forest Gâteau

Sieve the flour and cocoa powder together and gently fold into the mixture, using a metal spoon. Pour into a bottom-lined and greased 20-cm/8-in cake tin. Bake in a moderately hot oven (190 C, 375 F, gas 5) for 35-40 minutes. Turn out and cool on a wire tray.

To fill and decorate the gâteau, drain the juice from the cherries and blend a little with the arrowroot. Bring the remainder of the juice to the boil, then pour onto the blended arrowroot and return to the heat to thicken, stirring continuously. Add the cherries to the syrup and allow to cool.

Cut the cake in half and sprinkle the base with a little Kirsch. Whip the cream and with a nylon piping bag, fitted with a large star nozzle, pipe a circle of cream around the outside edge of the base. Fill the centre with half of the cherry mixture. Sprinkle the second layer of cake with a little Kirsch and place on top of the filling. Spread a little cream around the edge of the gâteau and press grated chocolate on top using a palette knife. Pipe swirls of cream on top of the gâteau and fill the centre with the remaining cherries. Sprinkle a little grated chocolate on the swirls of cream.

CHOCOLATE CHEESECAKE GÂTEAU

Biscuit base:
100 g/4 oz chocolate digestive biscuits
50 g/2 oz butter, melted
Filling:
225 g/8 oz cream cheese
100 g/4 oz caster sugar
2 eggs, separated
100 g/4 oz plain bitter
chocolate, melted
2 teaspoons gelatine
150 ml/¼ pint double cream, whipped
Decoration:
150 ml/¼ pint double cream
chocolate curls (page 73)
icing sugar

To make the biscuit base, crunch the biscuits into fine crumbs and stir in the melted butter. Press onto the base of an 18-cm/7-in springform tin and chill.

To make the filling, beat the cream cheese until smooth and add the sugar, egg yolks and melted chocolate. Dissolve the gelatine in two tablespoons of hot water and add to the cheese mixture. Whisk the egg whites until stiff and fold into the mixture. Then lastly fold in the whipped cream. Pour into the tin and chill until set.

To decorate the gâteau, whip the cream and, using a nylon piping bag, pipe a border around the edge. Decorate the centre with chocolate curls and sprinkle with icing sugar.

Helpful Hint. To crush biscuits, place them in a polythene bag and seal the open end. Use a rolling pin to crush the biscuits into crumbs, taking care not to burst the bag.

TROPICAL GÂTEAU

2 eggs
75 g/3 oz caster sugar
75 g/3 oz plain flour
2 tablespoons rum
Filling and Decoration:
1 small fresh pineapple
225 g/8 oz fresh dates
2 tablespoons rum
1 tablespoon soft brown sugar
300 ml/½ pint double cream
100 g/4 oz long thread coconut, lightly toasted
angelica leaves

Whisk the eggs with the sugar until pale and thick. Sieve the flour over the eggs and sprinkle over the rum. Fold in carefully using a metal spoon. Bottom-line and grease a Swiss roll tin measuring 18 × 28 cm/7 × 11 in. Turn the mixture into the tin and spread out evenly. Bake in a moderate oven (160C, 325F, gas 3) for 30-35 minutes. Turn out and cool on a wire tray, removing the greaseproof paper while the cake is still hot.

To fill and decorate the gâteau, slice and peel the pineapple then cut into neat pieces. Reserve approximately one-third of the pineapple for decoration. Stone and chop the dates. Mix the pineapple, dates and rum together. Sprinkle over the sugar and leave for at least 1 hour.

Slice the cake lengthways into two long, narrow, oblong pieces. Drain the juices off the fruit and sprinkle the juice over the pieces of cake. Arrange the fruit on one piece of cake and place the second piece on top. Whip the cream until stiff. Cover the sides and top of the cake thinly with cream and press the coconut against the sides of the cake using a palette knife. Place the remaining cream in a nylon piping bag, fitted with a large star nozzle, and pipe a line of cream down the middle of the cake. Arrange the reserved pineapple on either side of the cream and decorate with angelica leaves.

CREAMY PEACH MERINGUE

3 egg whites
175 g/6 oz caster sugar
50 g/2 oz plain chocolate, finely grated
Filling and Decoration:
3 large peaches
lemon juice
300 ml/½ pint double cream
chocolate curls (page 73)

Whisk the egg whites until stiff. Sprinkle over the caster sugar and whisk in vigorously until thick and glossy. Gently fold in the grated chocolate using a metal spoon. Bottom-line two 20-cm/8-in sandwich tins with non-stick baking parchment. Grease thoroughly. Divide the mixture between the two tins and smooth the top. Bake in a moderately hot oven (180C, 350F, gas 4) for 40-45 minutes. Allow to cool completely in the tins.

To fill and decorate the meringue, halve and stone the peaches. Remove the skin from one and a half peaches. Slice all the peaches thinly and sprinkle with a little lemon juice to prevent discoloration. Whip the cream until stiff. Carefully remove the baking parchment from the base of the cakes. Place one layer on the serving dish and spread half the cream over it. Arrange the peeled peach slices on top and sandwich with the remaining layer of cake. Spread the remaining cream on top and arrange unpeeled peach slices on the cake. Decorate with chocolate curls.

Creamy Peach Meringue and Tropical Gâteau

CHOUX GÂTEAU

150 ml/¼ pint water
50 g/2 oz butter
65 g/2½ oz plain flour, sieved
2 eggs
grated rind of 1 orange
25 g/1 oz flaked almonds
Filling and Decoration:
grated rind of ½ orange
juice of 1 orange
2 tablespoons sweet sherry
1 tablespoon thick honey
300 ml/½ pint double cream
icing sugar

Place the water and butter together in a saucepan and heat gently until the butter melts. Bring rapidly to the boil and add all the flour. Over the heat, beat thoroughly to form a smooth ball. Cool slightly then beat in the eggs individually, together with the orange rind. Place the paste in a nylon piping bag fitted with a 1-cm/½-in plain nozzle and pipe three small buns on a greased baking tray. Pipe the remaining mixture into a greased 20-cm/8-in sandwich tin and sprinkle the flaked almonds over the top. Bake the buns in a hot oven (220 C, 425 F, gas 7) for 10 minutes then reduce the temperature to 190 C, 375 F, gas 5 and cook for a further 10-15 minutes. Bake the main gâteau in a moderately hot oven (200 C, 400 F, gas 6) for 35 minutes then reduce the temperature to 190 C, 375 F, gas 5 and bake for a further 10-15 minutes. Split the buns and gâteau immediately and cool on a wire tray.

To fill and decorate the gâteau, stir together all the ingredients except the icing sugar and whip until stiff. Fill the buns and the main gâteau with the cream. Arrange the buns in the middle of the gâteau and sieve over a little icing sugar.

FRESH LIME GÂTEAU

50 g/2 oz caster sugar
2 eggs
50 g/2 oz plain flour
grated rind of 1 lime
caster sugar
Filling and Decoration:
300 ml/½ pint double cream
juice of ½ lime
slices of fresh lime

Whisk the sugar and eggs in a basin over a saucepan of hot water, until the mixture is thick and pale in colour.

Remove from the heat and continue to whisk until cool. Sieve the flour twice and fold into the whisked mixture with the rind of the lime. Place the mixture in a bottom-lined and greased 28 x 18-cm/11 x 7-in Swiss roll tin, smoothing over evenly. Bake in a moderately hot oven (200 C, 400 F, gas 6) for 8-10 minutes. Meanwhile, place a clean, damp tea-towel on a working surface, lay a sheet of greaseproof paper on top and sprinkle very lightly with caster sugar. Immediately the Swiss roll is cooked, turn out onto the sugared paper. Remove the lining paper and trim off the crusty edges. Make a shallow indentation with a knife along the narrow edge. Lay a sheet of clean greaseproof paper on top of the Swiss roll, then roll up tightly and cool.

To fill and decorate the gâteau, whip the cream with the lime juice. Carefully unroll the gâteau, and spread with some of the cream. Roll up and cover with the remaining cream, reserving some for piping. Use a palette knife to mark a design. Using a nylon piping bag, pipe cream down the centre and along the edges. Decorate with slices of lime.

Fresh Lime Gâteau

CHOCOLATE BRANDY SNAP GÂTEAU

3 eggs
75 g/3 oz caster sugar
65 g/2½ oz plain flour
15 g/½ oz cocoa powder
½ teaspoon baking powder
Filling and Decoration:
300 ml/½ pint double cream
1 (100-g/3·5-oz) packet
brandy snaps
ribbon
25 g/1 oz plain chocolate, melted

Place the eggs and sugar in a basin and whisk over a saucepan of hot water until thick and pale in colour. Remove from the heat and continue to whisk until cool. Sieve the flour, cocoa powder and baking powder together and gently fold into the mixture. Divide between two bottom-lined and greased 20-cm/8-in sandwich tins. Bake in a moderate oven (180 C, 350 F, gas 4) for 25-30 minutes. Turn out carefully and cool on a wire tray.

To decorate the gâteau, whip the cream and use a little to sandwich the cakes together. Spread a little around the sides, just enough to secure the brandy snaps around the edge of the cake. Tie a ribbon around the outside of the cake. Spread the remaining cream over the top of the cake, swirling with a palette knife. Place the melted chocolate in a greaseproof piping bag with a tiny hole cut in the point and drizzle over the cream and swirl with a skewer.

Helpful Hint. The cake can be prepared in advance but it is best to leave the decoration until 1-2 hours before serving otherwise the brandy snaps will become very soft.

HAZELNUT CREAM BOMBE

100 g/4 oz hazelnuts, finely chopped
3 eggs
175 g/6 oz caster sugar
150 g/5 oz plain flour
grated rind of 2 oranges
Filling and Decoration:
300 ml/½ pint double cream
2 tablespoons orange juice
2 tablespoons Cointreau
pared orange rind
orange slices
50 g/2 oz hazelnuts

Lightly toast the hazelnuts. Whisk the eggs with the sugar until pale and thick. Sieve the flour over the mixture and carefully fold in together with the hazelnuts and orange rind. Turn into a well greased 1·15-litre/2-pint pudding basin and bake in a moderate oven (180 C, 350 F, gas 4) for 45-50 minutes. Turn out and cool on a wire tray. Whip the cream with the orange juice and Cointreau until thick. Cut the cake into three, horizontally, and sandwich together with some of the cream. Reserve a third of the cream for piping and use the remainder to completely cover the bombe. Decorate with pared orange rind, orange slices, piped cream and hazelnuts.

WALNUT AND BANANA GALETTE

175 g/6 oz butter or margarine
100 g/4 oz caster sugar
grated rind of ½ lemon
175 g/6 oz plain flour
100 g/4 oz walnuts, chopped
Filling and Decoration:
300 ml/½ pint double cream
2 tablespoons icing sugar, sieved
4 bananas
lemon juice

Cream the butter, sugar and lemon rind until light and fluffy. Fold in the flour and knead together into a soft dough. Place in a polythene bag and chill for 30 minutes in the refrigerator. Divide the dough into three. Grease and flour three baking sheets and mark an 18-cm/7-in circle on each. Place a piece of dough in each circle and press out flat to fill the circle. Sprinkle the tops with the chopped walnuts and bake in a moderate oven (180 C, 350 F, gas 4) for 20-25 minutes. Allow to cool before turning out on to a wire tray.

To fill and decorate the galette, whip the cream and fold in the icing sugar. Slice the bananas, then sprinkle with a little lemon juice to prevent discoloration. Sandwich the layers with some cream and bananas. Using a nylon piping bag, pipe cream on top of the galette and decorate with slices of banana. Allow to stand for 30 minutes before serving.

MOCHA ROULADE

3 teaspoons instant coffee
1 tablespoon hot water
100 g/4 oz plain chocolate
4 eggs, separated
100 g/4 oz caster sugar
Decoration:
300 ml/½ pint double cream
little sifted icing sugar
chocolate shapes (page 73)

Blend the coffee with the hot water, add the chocolate and melt in a basin over a saucepan of hot water. Allow to cool. Whisk the egg yolks and sugar until stiff then fold into the mixture. Pour into a lined and greased 33 × 23-cm/13 × 9-in Swiss roll tin and bake in a moderate oven (180 C, 350 F, gas 4) for 15-20 minutes. Immediately after taking the cake out of the oven cover it (in the tin) with a damp tea-towel and leave covered overnight.

To decorate the roulade, carefully turn the cake out on to sugared paper, remove the lining paper. Whip the cream and spread over the cake, reserving a little for piping. Roll up like a Swiss roll and dust with the icing sugar. Pipe down the centre of the roll with the reserved cream and decorate with chocolate shapes.

Hazelnut Cream Bombe and Mocha Roulade

LOGANBERRY GÂTEAU

4 eggs
100 g/4 oz caster sugar
grated rind of ½ lemon
75 g/3 oz plain flour
25 g/1 oz cornflour
25 g/1 oz butter, melted
Filling and Decoration:
450 g/1 lb loganberries
6 tablespoons sherry
450 ml/¾ pint double cream, whipped
finely grated chocolate
loganberry or raspberry leaves

Place the eggs, sugar and lemon rind in a basin and whisk over a saucepan of hot water until pale and thick. Remove from the heat and continue to whisk until cool. Fold in the sieved flour and cornflour, and the melted butter, using a metal spoon. Pour into a bottom-lined and greased 20-cm/8-in square cake tin and bake in a moderately hot oven (190 C, 375 F, gas 5) for 30-35 minutes. Turn out and cool on a wire tray.

To fill and decorate the gâteau, reserve half the loganberries for decoration. Cut the cake into three, horizontally. Sprinkle the bottom layer with a little of the sherry and spread with some whipped cream, and a portion of the loganberries. Repeat with the second sponge layer on top. Top with the remaining sponge layer, cover the sides with a thin layer of cream and press the grated chcolate all over the sides with a palette knife. Cover the top with a thin layer of cream and, using a nylon piping bag, pipe a border of cream around the edges. Fill with the remaining loganberries and decorate with loganberry or raspberry leaves if available.

Helpful Hint. When loganberries are not in season you can use raspberries, strawberries or cherries in the gâteau.

heat. Shake the pan occasionally to allow the syrup to coat the almonds. Cook until the mixture turns a caramel colour. Pour into a greased tin and allow to set. Crush, using a rolling pin.

To fill and decorate the gâteau, whip the cream and mix sufficient cream and praline together to fill the gâteau. Sandwich the two layers together. Spread a little of the cream around the edge of the gâteau and press the praline onto the sides using a palette knife. Use the remaining cream to spread over the top and, using a nylon piping bag, pipe rosettes. Sprinkle with any remaining praline.

TIPSY RING

100 g/4 oz butter or margarine
100 g/4 oz caster sugar
5 tablespoons ginger wine
2 eggs
100 g/4 oz self-raising flour
25 g/1 oz cocoa powder
Icing and Decoration:
175 g/6 oz plain chocolate
50 g/2 oz butter
150 ml/¼ pint double cream
few pieces of crystallised ginger

Cream the butter with the sugar and 2 tablespoons ginger wine until pale and fluffy. Gradually, beat in the eggs. Sieve the flour with the cocoa powder and fold into the creamed mixture using a metal spoon. Turn into a well greased 23-cm/9-in ring tin and bake in a moderate oven (160 C, 325 F, gas 3) for 40-50 minutes. Turn out and cool on a wire tray. Whilst the cake is still warm, drizzle the remaining ginger wine over it, until absorbed.

To ice and decorate the ring, melt the chocolate with the butter. Allow to cool slightly then drizzle over the cake. Whip the cream until stiff and, using a nylon piping bag fitted with a large star nozzle, pipe the cream along the top of the cake. Decorate with pieces of crystallised ginger.

Variation

Use one tablespoon of coffee essence instead of the cocoa powder and rum instead of the ginger wine. Ice and decorate the cake as above.

Praline Gâteau

PRALINE GÂTEAU

100 g/4 oz caster sugar
3 eggs
75 g/3 oz plain flour
40 g/1 ½ oz butter or
margarine, melted
grated rind of 1 lemon
Praline:
100 g/4 oz split almonds
150 g/5 oz caster sugar
Filling and Decoration:
300 ml/½ pint double cream

Whisk the sugar and eggs in a basin over a saucepan of hot water until thick and creamy. Remove from the heat, continue to whisk until cool. Sieve the flour and fold into the whisked mixture with the butter and lemon rind, using a metal spoon. Divide the mixture between two bottom-lined and greased 20-cm/8-in sandwich tins. Bake in a moderately hot oven (180 C, 350 F, gas 4) for 15-20 minutes. Allow to cool slightly before turning out on to a wire tray.

To make the praline, place the almonds and sugar in a saucepan and allow the sugar to melt over a very low

Novelty Cakes

The cakes featured in this chapter are surprisingly easy to make and such fun for children's parties. The bases can be made in advance and frozen and some of the cakes can be frozen, iced, but without the final decorations. Remember to save any left-over trimmings. These can be frozen for future use, or used as a base for a trifle.

WINDMILL CAKE

350 g/12 oz plain flour
¼ teaspoon salt
225 g/8 oz butter or margarine
25 g/1 oz cocoa powder
100 g/4 oz caster sugar
1 egg yolk
¼ teaspoon almond essence
Icing and Decoration:
175 g/6 oz butter or margarine
275 g/10 oz icing sugar, sieved
few drops of almond essence
1 tablespoon cocoa powder
2 teaspoons boiling water
50 g/2 oz chocolate, grated
100 g/4 oz plain chocolate, melted
3 tablespoons icing sugar, sieved
¾ teaspoon boiling water
liquorice sweets
Smarties
almond paste (optional)

Sieve the flour and salt into a bowl. Add the butter and rub into the flour until the mixture resembles fine breadcrumbs. Add the sieved cocoa powder and sugar then mix to a dough with the egg yolk and almond essence. Form the dough into a roll of approximately 7·5 cm/3 in. in diameter, wrap in cling film and chill until firm. Cut into approximately eight slices and bake on a greased baking sheet in a moderately hot oven (190 C, 375 F, gas 5) for 15-20 minutes. Cool on a wire tray.

To ice and decorate the cake, cream the butter with the icing sugar until pale and fluffy. Divide the creamed mixture into two portions and flavour one with almond essence. Cream the cocoa powder with the boiling water and use to flavour the remaining cream. Add the grated chocolate to the chocolate cream. Sandwich the cooled biscuits together with the chocolate cream to form a tall pile. Chill until firm. Cover the outside completely with the almond cream.

Draw the shape of the sails on a piece of greaseproof paper. Carefully spread the melted chocolate within the outline leaving a small hole in the middle. Keep the layer even, not too thin and as smooth as possible. Similarly, draw and make chocolate windows and a door. Leave the chocolate shapes until firm and chill for an hour.

Mix the icing sugar with the water to give a smooth icing. Using a greaseproof piping bag with a tiny hole cut in the point, pipe the outline of the slats on the sails and the panes on the windows. When completely dry, carefully place one or two liquorice sweets on the end of a cocktail stick and use to attach the sails to the cake. Place the door and windows on the windmill. Arrange the Smarties on the top of the cake. Make almond paste flowers to put around the windmill, if liked.

Variation

If preferred, the windows and door may be made from almond paste (see page 70). Roll it out thinly and cut out the required shapes. The almond paste can also be tinted, before rolling out, with food colouring.

Windmill Cake

LOG CABIN

350 g/12 oz butter or margarine
350 g/12 oz caster sugar
6 eggs, lightly beaten
300 g/11 oz self-raising flour
50 g/2 oz cocoa powder
Icing and Decoration:
225 g/8 oz chocolate butter
icing (page 68)
2 (100-g/3·53-oz) packets chocolate
finger biscuits
100 g/4 oz almond paste, made-up
weight (page 70)*
2 tablespoons icing sugar, sieved
¾ teaspoon water
red food colouring
liquorice sweet

Cream the butter and sugar together until light and fluffy. Gradually, beat in the eggs together with 2 tablespoons of the flour. Sieve the remaining flour and cocoa powder over the mixture and fold in using a metal spoon. Spread the mixture evenly over a lined and greased 20-cm/8-in square cake tin. Bake in a moderate oven (160 C, 325 F, gas 3) for 2 hours. Turn out onto a wire tray, remove the greaseproof paper and leave to cool.

To ice and decorate the cake when cool, cut the top off the cake off the end to use for the roof. Cut the smaller piece of cake through diagonally to form two triangular-shaped pieces. Reserve two tablespoons of the butter icing for piping. Cover the top of the main piece of cake with butter icing and place the two pieces, ends together, on top for the roof. Cover the cake completely with butter icing, using slightly less on the roof than the sides.

Arrange the chocolate finger biscuits on the roof to resemble logs. Mark the sides of the cake horizontally using a round-bladed knife to give the effect of a log cabin. Roll out the almond paste and cut out a door and windows. Mix the icing sugar with the water to form a thick glacé icing. Paint the door using a greaseproof piping bag with a tiny hole cut in the point, pipe glacé icing for the features. Place a liquorice sweet on top of the roof for the chimney. Sieve a little icing sugar onto the roof to represent snow.

*If preferred, you can use ready-prepared almond paste available from most supermarkets.

Variation

For a nutty cake, omit the cocoa powder and use 350 g/ 12 oz self-raising flour. Fold in 100 g/4 oz chopped walnuts with the remaining flour. Bake as for the chocolate cake.

TREASURE CHEST

175 g/6 oz butter or margarine
175 g/6 oz caster sugar
grated rind of 2 oranges
3 eggs
200 g/7 oz self-raising flour
juice of 1 orange
Icing and Decoration:
175 g/6 oz plain chocolate
50 g/2 oz butter
100 g/4 oz orange butter icing (page 68)
variety of small sweets

Cream the butter with the sugar until pale and fluffy. Carefully beat in the orange rind and eggs. Sieve the flour over the mixture and fold in gently using a metal spoon. Lastly fold in the orange juice. Turn into a lined and greased 1-kg/2-lb loaf tin and bake in a moderate oven (160 C, 325 F, gas 3) for approximately 1½ hours. Turn out and cool on a wire tray.

To ice and decorate the cake, melt the chocolate with the butter in a basin over a pan of hot water. Slice

Cuthbert Car

the top off the cake and reserve as the lid. Cover the whole of the cake thinly with the chocolate. When the chocolate is set, place the butter icing in a piping bag fitted with a small star nozzle and pipe an edge around the cake. Pipe designs around the sides and top of the cake. Place the various sweets as 'treasure' on top of the cake, arranging some to hand over the edge. Arrange the lid, tilting slightly backwards, on top of the cake.

CUTHBERT CAR

1 (23 x 33-cm/9 x 13-in) sandwich cake
(boat cake, page 57)
Icing and Decoration:
225 g/8 oz lemon curd
1 (25-cm/10-in) square cake board,
in silver
225 g/8 oz butter icing (page 68)
green food colouring
Smarties
chocolate buttons

To ice and decorate the car, cut the cake in half widthways and sandwich the two pieces together with a little of the lemon curd. Place on the cake board. Mix the remaining lemon curd with the butter icing. Cut out a piece of greaseproof paper the same size as the cake. Draw the shape of the car on the paper, place on top of the cake and use as an outline to cut out the car. Cut out the wheels from the offcuts.

Reserve 3 tablespoons of the icing and use the remainder to cover the cake completely. Mark the icing by using a round-bladed knife. Colour the reserved icing green and pipe the features on the cake using a greaseproof piping bag with a small hole cut in the point. Place red and yellow Smarties on the cake to represent lights and chocolate buttons for hubcaps.

BASKET CAKE

*1 Victoria sandwich, made with
175 g/6 oz butter or margarine
175 g/6 oz caster sugar
3 eggs
175 g/6 oz self-raising flour (page 16)*
Icing and Decoration:
*350 g/12 oz chocolate butter
icing (see opposite)
1 (23-cm/9-in) silver cake board
sweets*

Make up the Victoria sandwich cake, as directed, and place in a lined and greased 20-cm/8-in cake tin. Bake in a moderate oven (160 C, 325 F, gas 3) for 1-1¼ hours. Turn out and cool on a wire tray. Cut a slice horizontally across the top of the cake to form the lid.

To ice and decorate the cake, make up the chocolate butter icing as directed. Place the cake on the silver cake board and cover with a thin layer of the icing. Fill two greaseproof piping bags with the icing, one fitted with a plain writing nozzle and the other with a ribbon nozzle. Holding the ribbon nozzle sideways on to the cake, pipe three lines, evenly spaced one above the other, and all the same length. Pipe a vertical line using the writing tube along the edge of the basket weaving. Continue this process until the cake is covered. Cover the outer edge of the lid in the same way. Arrange the lid at an angle on top of the cake to form an open basket. Fill the inside with sweets.

Helpful Hint. This cake would make a welcome gift for Mother's Day or for an elderly person. Buy a box of the person's favourite sweets or chocolates to put on top of the cake. For Easter top the cake with small chocolate eggs.

BOOK CAKE

*1 (23 x 33-cm/9 x 13-in) sandwich cake
(boat cake, page 57)*
Icing and Decoration:
*225 g/8 oz butter icing (page 68)
50 g/2 oz plain chocolate, melted
1 piece of coloured ribbon*

To ice and decorate the cake, cover the cake completely in butter icing, reserving about one-third for piping. Place the reserved butter icing in a piping bag fitted with a small star nozzle and pipe the edges around the cake. Use a small greaseproof piping bag with a tiny hole cut in its point to pipe the features on the cake in melted chocolate to resemble a book. Arrange the ribbon down the middle of the cake to form a bookmark.

Helpful Hint. This cake also makes an excellent treat for adults. Pipe the name of a favourite book, film or programme on the cake along with the name of the person who is celebrating a birthday.

For ease and speed, you can always use a shop-bought cake instead of preparing your own.

Basket Cake

CHOCOLATE CLOCK CAKE

1 (20-cm/8-in) chocolate Victoria sandwich cake (page 16)
Icing and Decoration:
225 g/8 oz fudge icing (page 68)
50 g/2 oz icing sugar
about 1 tablespoon hot water
chocolate buttons
50 g/2 oz plain chocolate, melted
ribbon

To ice and decorate the cake, sandwich the cake together using one-third of the fudge icing. Spread the remaining icing over the top and sides of the cake. Sieve the icing sugar into a small basin and mix gradually with the water to give a smooth glacé icing. Using a grease-proof piping bag, with a tiny hole cut in the point, pipe the numbers 1 to 12 on the chocolate buttons and a spiral on the button that is to go in the middle of the cake. Place the buttons around the edge of the cake to resemble a clock and the one with the spiral in the middle.

Draw the shape of the hands for the clock on a piece of greaseproof paper. Carefully spread the melted chocolate within the outline of the drawing, making it as thick and as smooth as possible. Leave in a cool place until set. Tie a ribbon around the side of the cake and place the hands on the clock face, pointing them to the number which is appropriate for the age of the child whose birthday is being celebrated or any other number which is relevant to the celebration.

ALPHABET STACK

1 (23 x 33-cm/9 x 13-in) sandwich cake (boat cake, page 57)
Icing and Decoration:
175 g/6 oz plain chocolate
100 g/4 oz butter or margarine
225 g/8 oz icing sugar, sieved
1-2 tablespoons lemon juice
100 g/4 oz almond paste, made-up weight, (page 70)*
food colouring

To ice and decorate the cake, trim the edges off the cake. Melt the chocolate and butter together. Gradually beat in the icing sugar and lemon juice to give an icing of a soft consistency, similar to that of a firm butter icing. Add a little more lemon juice if necessary. The icing will need vigorous beating to obtain a soft consistency and will harden as it cools. Spread the icing over the top of the cake and leave until almost set. Using a sharp, wet knife, cut the cake into four, both widthways and lengthways to give 16 pieces of cake. Knead the almond paste slightly then roll out thinly on a clean surface, sprinkled with sieved icing sugar. Using a small, sharp pointed knife, cut out the almond paste in the shape of the letters, making them approximately 3·5 cm/ 1½-2 in. in height. Using a small artists' paintbrush or pastry brush, colour the letters with various diluted food colours. Leave until dry, then place on the pieces of cake and leave until the icing is quite firm. Arrange in a stack or in the name of a child.

Chocolate Clock Cake

BUS CAKE

175 g/6 oz butter or margarine
175 g/6 oz caster sugar
grated rind of 2 lemons
juice of 1 lemon
3 eggs, beaten
225 g/8 oz self-raising flour
Icing and Decoration:
225 g/8 oz lemon butter icing (page 68)
yellow food colouring
75 g/3 oz plain chocolate, melted
50 g/2 oz icing sugar
1 tablespoon hot water
Smarties
2 mini chocolate rolls
100 g/4 oz plain chocolate,
grated (optional)

Cream the butter with the sugar and lemon rind until light and fluffy. Beat in the lemon juice and gradually beat in the eggs. Sieve the flour over the mixture and carefully fold in using a metal spoon. Turn into a lined and greased 1·5-kg/3-lb loaf tin and bake in a moderate oven (160 C, 325 F, gas 3) for 1¼-1½ hours. Turn out and cool on a wire tray. When cool, level off the top of the cake and cut out a piece, approximately

2·5 x 3·5 cm/1 x 1½ in from one end of the cake to form the engine shape.

To ice and decorate the cake, reserve two table-spoons of the butter icing. Colour the remainder yellow and cover the cake completely. Cream the melted chocolate with the reserved butter icing. Place in a greaseproof piping bag with a tiny hole cut in the point and pipe the features on the bus. Mix the icing sugar with the water to give a smooth glacé icing and pipe faces on the Smarties. Place these in the windows. Halve the mini rolls and place under the cake for the wheels. Place on a board and surround with grated chocolate, if liked.

NUMERAL CAKE

*1 (20-cm/8-in) Victoria sandwich cake
(page 16)*
Icing and Decoration:
*450 g/1 lb butter icing (page 68)
food colouring
coloured sweets or
chocolate buttons
candles*

Cut out two 20-cm/8-in rounds of greaseproof paper, overlap slightly at one end and pin together. Draw the shape of the figure 3 on the two pieces of paper and mark a dotted line at the point where they overlap. Use as much of the area as possible when drawing the numeral. Unpin the pieces of paper and cut out the shapes which have been drawn. Use these as a pattern to cut out the shape from the two pieces of cake.

To ice and decorate the cake, fit the cake together on a board. Colour the butter cream as desired. Reserve a quarter of the butter cream for piping and use the remainder to cover the cake completely. Using a greaseproof piping bag fitted with a small rosette or star nozzle, pipe an edge around the cake. Decorate with the sweets and place the appropriate number of candles on the cake.

Variations

Using the same method, that is cutting out paper patterns first, other numerals may be cut out of the cake. For some of the smaller numbers, the cake may be sandwiched together first. A figure eight may simply be made by cutting out a 7·5-cm/3-in round from the middle of each piece of cake. The ends of the two pieces should be cut off slightly where they fit together. A figure six may be cut out of the cake which has already been sandwiched together.

CHOCOLATE HEDGEHOGS

M A K E S   6

*225 g/8 oz plain flour
100 g/4 oz butter or margarine
75 g/3 oz caster sugar
grated rind of 2 oranges
3 tablespoons orange juice
275 g/10 oz chocolate cake crumbs
3 tablespoons lemon jelly marmalade, warmed
50 g/2 oz butter, melted
1 tablespoon melted chocolate*

Numeral Cake

5 tablespoons orange juice
Icing and Decoration:
*50 g/2 oz blanched almonds
225 g/8 oz plain chocolate, melted*

Sieve the flour into a bowl, add the butter and rub in lightly until the mixture resembles fine breadcrumbs. Add the sugar and orange rind and mix to form a dough using the orange juice. Knead lightly then roll out to 5 mm/¼ in thickness. Cut out six oval shapes measuring 10 x 6 cm/4 x 2½ in. Place on greased baking trays and bake in a moderately hot oven (190 C, 375 F, gas 5) for 12-15 minutes. Cool on a wire tray.

Meanwhile, mix together the remaining ingredients. Chill until the mixture is firm enough to shape with the hands. Pile this mixture on top of the cooled orange bases and smooth into domes. Shape the front to form bases and smooth into domes. Shape the front to form noses. Chill until firm.

To ice and decorate the cakes, quarter the almonds lengthwise and stick into the hedgehogs to resemble spines. Reserve a few pieces of the almonds for eyes and noses. Coat the hedgehogs completely in melted chocolate and leave until firm. When the chocolate is half-set, place small pieces of almond on the front to form eyes and a nose.

BOAT CAKE

175 g/6 oz butter or margarine
175 g/6 oz caster sugar
few drops of vanilla essence
3 eggs, lightly beaten
175 g/6 oz self-raising flour
3 tablespoons strawberry jam
Icing and Decoration:
225 g/8 oz butter icing (page 68)
red food colouring
1 liquorice sweet
few bought chocolate sticks

Cream the butter and sugar together until light and fluffy. Gradually beat in the vanilla essence with the eggs. Sieve the flour over the mixture and fold in using a metal spoon. Spread evenly over a bottom-lined and greased 23 x 33-cm/9 x 13-in Swiss roll tin and bake in a moderate oven (180C, 350F, gas 4) for 20-25 minutes. Turn out onto a wire tray, remove the greaseproof paper and leave to cool. Cut a strip approximately 5 cm/2 in. in width off the narrow edge of the cake. Halve the remaining cake widthwise and sandwich together with most of the jam. Halve the strip along the edge and sandwich together using the remaining jam. Cut the shape of the boat from the main piece of cake, measuring 13 cm/5 in wide at one end shaped to a point at the other. Cut one end of the small piece of cake to a point and place on top of the main cake, to form the cabin.

To ice and decorate the cake, colour half the butter icing red. Reserve two tablespoons of each portion of butter icing for piping. Cover the main part of the cake in white butter icing and the cabin in red. Using a greaseproof piping bag with a tiny hole cut in the point, pipe the remaining features on the cake. Place the liquorice sweet as the funnel on top of the cabin and chocolate sticks around the edge.

Small Cakes

Small cakes are always in demand, for teas and parties or even as gifts. This chapter includes a wide variety of recipes from the simple to the sophisticated – ideas which will be a roaring success with both adults and children alike.

CHOCOLATE SHORTBREAD HEARTS

MAKES 22 TO 24

175 g/6 oz butter
75 g/3 oz caster sugar
225 g/8 oz plain flour
25 g/1 oz cocoa powder
Icing and Decoration:
100 g/4 oz chocolate butter
icing (page 68)
175 g/6 oz plain chocolate, melted

Cream the butter and sugar together until pale and fluffy. Sieve the flour with the cocoa powder and beat into the creamed mixture to give a soft dough. Chill, knead lightly and roll out thinly. Use a heart-shaped biscuit cutter to cut out the biscuits and place on greased baking trays. Bake in a moderate oven (160 C, 325 F, gas 3) for 15 minutes. Cool slightly on the baking trays then remove to wire trays and leave until cold.

To ice and decorate the biscuits, use a small star nozzle to pipe around the edge of the biscuits with chocolate butter icing. Pour the chocolate into the centre of the biscuits and allow to cool.

MERINGUES

MAKES 12 TO 13 PAIRS

2 egg whites
100 g/4 oz caster sugar
Filling and Decoration:
300 ml/½ pint double cream
few glacé cherries
angelica leaves

Whisk the egg whites until stiff. Gradually whisk in half the sugar then carefully fold in the remainder using a metal spoon. Transfer the mixture to a piping bag fitted with a large star nozzle and pipe small meringues on to greased baking trays. Dry out in a very cool oven (110 C, 225 F, gas ¼), or at the lowest setting to which the oven may be turned, for 3½-4 hours. Remove and cool on a wire tray.

To fill and decorate the meringues, whip the cream until stiff and use to sandwich the meringues together, either by piping through a larger star nozzle or by using a spoon. Decorate with pieces of cherry and angelica leaves.

Chocolate Shortbread Hearts

HONEY SQUARES

MAKES 12

175 g/6 oz thick honey
175 g/6 oz butter or margarine
75 g/3 oz demerara sugar
100 g/4 oz sultanas
75 g/3 oz blanched almonds, chopped
grated rind of 2 oranges
juice of ½ orange
2 eggs, lightly beaten
200 g/7 oz self-raising flour
1 teaspoon baking powder
½ teaspoon ground cinnamon
Topping:
100 g/4 oz blanched almonds
5 tablespoons thick honey
50 g/2 oz sultanas
generous pinch of ground cinnamon
grated rind of 1 orange

Melt the honey, butter and sugar together with the sultanas, almonds, orange rind and juice over a gentle heat. Cool slightly, then beat in the eggs. Sieve together the dry ingredients and beat into the mixture to give a smooth batter. Pour into a lined and greased 18 x 26-cm/7 x 10½-in shallow tin and bake in a

Honey Squares and Lemon Honey Buns (overleaf)

moderate oven (160 C, 325 F, gas 3) for 40-50 minutes. Cool slightly in the tin then mix together all the ingredients for the topping. Warm slightly, if necessary, then spread over the top of the cake and leave to cool. Cut into squares when cold.

Helpful Hint. When weighing honey, first lightly flour the scale pan, then spoon in the honey. It can then be transferred quite easily to the saucepan leaving a clean scale pan.

LEMON HONEY BUNS
MAKES 12 TO 14

100 g/4 oz butter or margarine
50 g/2 oz soft brown sugar
100 g/4 oz thick honey
grated rind and juice of 1 lemon
2 eggs, lightly beaten
225 g/8 oz self-raising flour
1 teaspoon baking powder
Icing and Decoration:
225 g/8 oz lemon glacé icing (page 68)
pared lemon rind

Melt the butter, sugar and honey together with the lemon rind and juice over a gentle heat, stirring occasionally. Leave to cool slightly. Beat in the eggs. Sieve the flour and baking powder together and beat thoroughly into the melted mixture to give a smooth thick batter.

Divide between greased, deep patty tins and bake in a moderately hot oven (190 C, 375 F, gas 5) for 15-20 minutes. Cool on a wire tray.

Decorate with glacé icing and pieces of pared lemon rind.

BROWNIES
MAKES 16 TO 18

50 g/2 oz self-raising flour
½ teaspoon baking powder
40 g/1½ oz cocoa powder
25 g/1 oz ground almonds
225 g/8 oz soft brown sugar
grated rind of 1 orange
100 g/4 oz butter or margarine, softened
2 eggs, lightly beaten
Icing:
100 g/4 oz plain chocolate
25 g/1 oz butter or margarine
50 g/2 oz blanched almonds, chopped

Sieve the flour, baking powder and cocoa powder into a bowl. Add the ground almonds, sugar and orange rind and mix together well. Beat the butter and eggs into the dry ingredients until smooth. Spread the mixture evenly in a lined and greased 18-cm/7-in square, shallow tin. Bake in a moderate oven (160 C, 325 F, gas 3) for 50-55 minutes. Allow to cool in the tin.

To ice the brownies, melt the chocolate with the butter then stir in the chopped almonds. Spread the icing evenly over the brownies then cut into small squares when half set.

ICED FANCIES
MAKES APPROX 30

1 (23 x 33-cm/9 x 13-in) Genoese sponge cake (page 18)
Icing and Decoration:
225 g/8 oz glacé icing (page 68)
food colourings
175 g/6 oz butter icing (page 68)
various small sweets, cake decorations
chocolate buttons or vermicelli

Cut the cake into small squares, diamonds and oblong shapes. A biscuit cutter may be used to cut out rounds of cake, but this does produce wasted cuttings.

To ice and decorate the fancies, the glacé icing may be coloured in any selection of colours. Divide the icing into several portions and add a few drops of food colouring to each. The colour should be delicate. Cover the cake shapes in glacé icing and leave to set slightly. Similarly, the butter icing should be delicately coloured and then placed in a piping bag fitted with a small star nozzle. The cakes may be decorated with piped butter icing and various sweets as shown in the picture. Alternatively, the sides of the cakes can be spread with butter icing and coated in grated chocolate, chopped nuts, coconut or sugar strands as preferred. The top of the cakes should be iced with glacé icing and decorated with piped butter icing.

Iced Fancies and Coffee Butterflies (overleaf)

FAIRY CAKES
MAKES 18 TO 20

100 g/4 oz butter or margarine
100 g/4 oz caster sugar
2 eggs
150 g/5 oz self-raising flour
Icing and Decoration:
225 g/8 oz glacé icing (page 68)
few drops of food colouring
small sweets or nuts

Cream the butter and sugar together until pale and fluffy. Gradually, beat in the eggs then sieve the flour over the mixture and fold in gently using a metal spoon. Place the mixture in greased patty tins or paper cake cases placed on a baking tray and bake in a moderate oven (180 C, 350 F, gas 4) for 15-20 minutes. Turn out of the patty tins and cool on a wire tray.

To ice and decorate the cakes, colour the glacé icing delicately in any preferred colour and use to cover the top of the cakes. The iced cakes may be decorated with various sweets or nuts as shown in the picture.

Variations
Chocolate cup cakes Add 2 tablespoons cocoa powder to the flour. Decorate the cakes with 175 g/ 6 oz melted plain chocolate or glacé icing with melted chocolate drizzled on top.

Nutty buns Add 50 g/2 oz mixed dried fruit or chopped glacé cherries to the mixture. Mix 100 g/4 oz sieved icing sugar with 1-2 tablespoons sherry to give a smooth icing. Drizzle the icing over the top of the cakes.

COFFEE BUTTERFLIES
MAKES 18 TO 20

100 g/4 oz butter or margarine
100 g/4 oz caster sugar
2 eggs
100 g/4 oz self-raising flour
1 tablespoon coffee essence
Icing and Decoration:
225 g/8 oz coffee butter icing (page 68)
50 g/2 oz plain chocolate, melted

Cream the butter with the sugar until pale and fluffy. Gradually, beat in the eggs then sieve the flour over the mixture and fold in gently using a metal spoon. Fold in the coffee essence. Place the mixture in greased bun tins or paper cake cases placed on a baking tray and bake in a moderate oven (180 C, 350 F, gas 4) for 15-20

minutes. Cool on a wire tray.

To ice and decorate the cakes, slice the tops off the cakes and cut them in half to form semi-circles. Place the butter icing in a piping bag fitted with a small star nozzle and pipe swirls on top of the cut cakes. Place the melted chocolate in a greaseproof piping bag, cut a tiny hole in the point and pipe patterns on each of the semi-circles. When the chocolate is set, press the pieces of cake into the swirls of butter icing to form wings.

Fairy Cakes

NUTTY ANGELICA FANCIES
MAKES 12

100 g/4 oz butter or magarine
100 g/4 oz caster sugar
2 eggs, lightly beaten
100 g/4 oz self-raising flour, sieved
100 g/4 oz walnuts, chopped
75 g/3 oz angelica, chopped
Icing and Decoration:
225 g/8 oz glacé icing (page 68)
25 g/1 oz walnuts, chopped
50 g/2 oz angelica, chopped

Cream the butter with the sugar until light and fluffy. Gradually, beat in the eggs and fold in the flour using a metal spoon. Mix together the walnuts and angelica and fold into the cake mixture. Divide the mixture between 12 greased dariole moulds and bake in a moderate oven (180 C, 350 F, gas 4) for 25-30 minutes. Turn out and cool on a wire tray.

To ice and decorate the cakes, drizzle the glacé icing over the top of each cake and sprinkle with a mixture of chopped walnuts and angelica.

Nutty Angelica Fancies

MINTY CHOCOLATE CUPS
MAKES 24

100 g/4 oz butter or margarine
100 g/4 oz caster sugar
¼ teaspoon peppermint essence
2 eggs, lightly beaten
100 g/4 oz self-raising flour
100 g/4 oz plain chocolate, grated
Icing and Decoration:
225 g/8 oz plain chocolate, melted
crystallised mint leaves (page 74)

Cream the butter with the sugar until light and fluffy. Gradually beat in the peppermint essence and eggs. Sieve the flour over the mixture and fold in using a metal spoon. Lastly fold in the grated chocolate. Divide the mixture between 24 paper cake cases placed on a baking tray or in patty tins and bake in a moderately hot oven (190 C, 375 F, gas 5) for 20 minutes. Cool on a wire tray.

When cold, spread the tops with chocolate and decorate with a few crystallised mint leaves.

MOCHA ROUND

MAKES 20 TO 24 SLICES

75 g/3 oz golden syrup
50 g/2 oz butter
grated rind of 1 orange and
juice of ½ orange
grated rind of 1 lemon
75 g/3 oz sultanas
100 g/4 oz glacé cherries,
roughly chopped
2 teaspoons coffee essence
2 tablespoons ginger wine
75 g/3 oz blanched almonds, chopped
225 g/8 oz plain chocolate digestive
biscuits, crushed
75 g/3 oz ground almonds
Coating:
100 g/4 oz blanched almonds, chopped

Place all the ingredients, except the biscuits and ground almonds in a saucepan over a low heat. Stir continuously until completely melted and combined, then bring to the boil and cook for 1 minute. Stir in the digestive biscuits and ground almonds and leave in a cool place until firm enough to shape into a long roll, approximately 5 cm/2 in. in diameter and 23-25 cm/9-10 in. in length.

To coat the roll, roll in the chopped blanched almonds until completely coated. Wrap in foil or cling film and chill until quite firm. Cut into slices before serving.

BANANA DATE FINGERS

MAKES 18

100 g/4 oz butter or margarine
50 g/2 oz caster sugar
1 egg yolk
100 g/4 oz self-raising flour
100 g/4 oz ground almonds
Filling:
4 bananas (about 675 g/1 ½ lb unpeeled weight)
juice of 1 lemon
225 g/8 oz dates, stoned and halved
50 g/2 oz blanched almonds, halved
3 tablespoons soft brown sugar
Topping:
1 egg
50 g/2 oz soft brown sugar
25 g/1 oz plain flour

50 g/2 oz ground almonds
icing sugar

Cream the butter with the sugar until pale and fluffy. Beat in the egg yolk then stir in the flour and ground almonds to form a very soft dough. Press into the base of a greased 18 × 28-cm/7 × 11-in Swiss roll tin and prick all over with a fork. Bake blind in a moderately hot oven (160 C, 325 F, gas 3) for 30-40 minutes. Cool slightly.

To make the filling, slice the bananas then sprinkle with the lemon juice, mixing well. Add the remaining ingredients. Stir well and arrange evenly over the base.

To make the topping, whisk the egg with the sugar until thick and creamy. Sieve the flour over the egg mixture and fold in carefully with the ground almonds. Spread this mixture thinly and evenly over the bananas and dates. Bake in a moderately hot oven (190 C, 375 F, gas 5) for 40 minutes, until golden in colour. Cool in the tin and cut into fingers when cold. Sieve icing sugar over the tops before serving.

Banana Date Fingers

CRUNCHY COFFEE CAKES

MAKES 18 TO 20

Base and topping:
100 g/4 oz plain flour
50 g/2 oz butter or margarine
75 g/3 oz soft brown sugar
100 g/4 oz brazil nuts, chopped
Cake mixture:
100 g/4 oz butter or margarine
100 g/4 oz caster sugar
2 eggs
100 g/4 oz self-raising flour
2 tablespoons instant coffee granules

To make the base and topping, sieve the flour into a bowl and rub in the butter until the mixture resembles fine breadcrumbs. Add the sugar and chopped nuts and stir together well. Press half of this mixture over the base of a greased 28×18-cm/11×7-in Swiss roll tin.

To make the cake mixture, cream the butter with the sugar until pale and fluffy. Beat in the eggs and sieve the flour over the mixture. Fold in lightly using a metal spoon. Lastly, lightly stir in the instant coffee granules.

Crunchy Coffee Cakes and Chocolate Marble Squares (overleaf)

Spread this mixture evenly over the base and sprinkle the remaining nut mixture on top. Bake in a moderate oven (160 C, 325 F, gas 3) for approximately 1 hour, or until golden brown in colour and firm to the touch. Leave to cool in the tin then cut into pieces and carefully remove from the tin.

Helpful Hint. If you are worried about the cake sticking to the baking tin, then it is always a good idea to line the base with greaseproof paper before greasing the tin.

APPLE AND GINGER RINGS

MAKES 9

2 eggs
100 g/4 oz golden syrup
1 medium cooking apple (about 175 g/6 oz)
juice of 1 lemon
1 piece preserved stem ginger, chopped
100 g/4 oz self-raising flour
¼ teaspoon ground ginger
Icing and Decoration:
100 g/4 oz icing sugar
1-2 tablespoons ginger wine
crystallised ginger
small pieces of apple, dipped in lemon juice

Whisk the eggs with the syrup until pale and thick. Peel, core and grate the apple, sprinkle with the lemon juice and mix with the preserved stem ginger. Fold this apple mixture into the eggs. Sieve the flour and ginger together and fold into the egg mixture.

Divide the mixture between nine well-greased 11-cm/4½-in ring tins and bake in a moderately hot oven (190 C, 375 F, gas 5) for 20-25 minutes. Turn out and cool on a wire tray.

To ice and decorate the rings, sieve the icing sugar into a bowl and mix to a smooth consistency with the ginger wine. Drizzle the icing over the cooled cakes and decorate with crystallised ginger and small pieces of apple.

CHOCOLATE MARBLE SQUARES

MAKES 25

175 g/6 oz butter or margarine
175 g/6 oz caster sugar
3 eggs
175 g/6 oz self-raising flour
¼ teaspoon almond essence
2 tablespoons cocoa powder
2 tablespoons boiling water
Icing and Decoration:
225 g/8 oz glacé icing (page 68)
few drops of almond essence
chocolate curls (page 73)

Cream the butter with the sugar until pale and fluffy. Gradually beat in the eggs then sieve the flour and fold in carefully using a metal spoon. Divide the mixture in

Apple and Ginger Rings

half and flavour one portion with the almond essence. Cream the cocoa powder with the boiling water, cool slightly and beat into the other portion of cake mixture.

Place small spoonfuls of the mixture at random in a lined and greased 25-cm/10-in square shallow tin and swirl the two mixtures together slightly. Bang the tin sharply on the table to even out the mixture and bake in a moderate oven (160 C, 325 F, gas 3) for 1 hour and 5 minutes, or until risen and firm to the touch. Turn out, remove the lining paper and cool on a wire tray.

To ice and decorate the squares, cut the cake into 25 squares. Flavour the glacé icing with a few drops of almond essence and spread over the top of the squares. Decorate with chocolate curls.

LEMON MAIDS

MAKES 18

Pastry:
225 g/8 oz plain flour
100 g/4 oz butter or margarine
grated rind of 2 lemons
40 g/1½ oz caster sugar
1 tablespoon cold water
4 tablespoons lemon curd

Sponge Topping:
75 g/3 oz softened butter or margarine
75 g/3 oz caster sugar
75 g/3 oz self-raising flour
25 g/1 oz ground almonds
1 egg, lightly beaten
3 tablespoons lemon juice

Icing and Decoration:
175 g/6 oz lemon curd
75 g/3 oz ground almonds
coarsely grated or pared lemon rind

To make the pastry, sieve the flour into a bowl, add the butter and rub in until the mixture resembles fine breadcrumbs. Add the lemon rind, sugar and water and mix to a smooth dough. Knead lightly then roll out thinly. Cut out eighteen 6-7·5-cm/2½-3-in rounds and use to line patty tins. Place a little of the lemon curd in each pastry case then leave in a cool place while making the sponge topping.

To make the sponge topping, place all the ingredients for the topping in a bowl and beat well until pale and fluffy. Place enough of this mixture in each pastry case to reach almost to the top. Bake in a moderate oven (180 C, 350 F, gas 4) for approximately 20 minutes, until risen and golden. Turn out and cool on a wire tray.

To ice and decorate the cakes, mix the lemon curd with the ground almonds and spread over the cooled cakes. Decorate with a little lemon rind.

Icing & Decoration

With the clear and precise, step-by-step instructions detailed in this chapter, you will be able to achieve a professional finish on all your decorated cakes. Turn melted chocolate into chocolate leaves, or royal icing into moulded flowers to give that professional touch and to impress your friends with your masterpieces.

BUTTER ICING

Makes 225 g/8 oz butter icing, sufficient to fill and ice the top and sides of a 20-cm/8-in sandwich cake.

75 g/3 oz butter or margarine
225 g/8 oz icing sugar
2 tablespoons milk
food colouring (optional)

Place all the ingredients in a mixing bowl and beat together with a wooden spoon until well mixed.

Variations
Orange or lemon icing Substitute the milk for orange or lemon juice.
Coffee icing Replace 1 tablespoon milk with 1 tablespoon coffee essence or 1 tablespoon instant coffee dissolved in 1 tablespoon of boiling water. Cool before adding to the icing.
Chocolate icing Replace 1 tablespoon milk with 1 tablespoon cocoa powder, blended with 2 tablespoons hot water.
Mocha icing Add 1 tablespoon coffee essence and 1 tablespoon cocoa powder blended with 2 tablespoons hot water.

FUDGE ICING

Makes 225 g/8 oz of fudge icing sufficient to fill and ice the top and sides of a 20-cm/8-in sandwich cake.

50 g/2 oz butter or margarine
3 tablespoons milk
225 g/8 oz icing sugar, sieved

Place all the ingredients in a basin over a saucepan of hot water. Stir until smooth and glossy. Remove from the heat and allow to cool. Beat well with a wooden spoon until the mixture is thick enough to spread.

Variations
Lemon or orange fudge icing Replace 2 tablespoons milk with 2 tablespoons orange or lemon juice.
Coffee fudge icing Replace 1 tablespoon milk with 1 tablespoon instant coffee dissolved in 1 tablespoon of boiling water.
Chocolate fudge icing Use only 1 tablespoon milk and 2 tablespoons hot water blended with 1 tablespoon cocoa powder.

GLACÉ ICING

Makes 225 g/8 oz glacé icing, sufficient to ice 18-20 small cakes or the top of a 20-cm/8-in cake.

225 g/8 oz icing sugar, sieved
2-3 tablespoons water
food colouring (optional)

Place all ingredients in a mixing bowl and beat with a wooden spoon until smooth.

Variations
Orange, lemon or lime glacé icing Replace the water with fresh fruit juice or fruit squash.
Coffee glacé icing Replace 1 tablespoon of the water with 1 tablespoon coffee essence or 1 teaspoon instant coffee dissolved in 1 tablespoon hot water.
Chocolate glacé icing Sieve 2 tablespoons cocoa powder with the icing sugar, adding a little more water if necessary.

FONDANT ICING

Makes 350 g/12 oz fondant icing, sufficient to cover an 18-cm/7-in round or a 15-cm/6-in square cake.

350 g/12 oz icing sugar, sieved
1 egg white
1 tablespoon liquid glucose, warmed
icing sugar
egg white, to brush cake

Place the icing sugar, egg white and glucose in a mixing bowl and mix together using a palette knife. Knead together with the fingertips until a dough is formed. Turn out on to a board, well dredged with icing sugar and knead until easy to handle. Roll out the dough approximately 5 cm/2 in larger than the surface of the cake to be iced. Brush the cake with egg white, place the icing on top of the cake and smooth the icing quickly using fingers dipped in cornflour, easing the icing down the sides of the cake. Trim the icing at the base and allow to harden before decorating. Do not store in an airtight tin. This icing can be used for moulding, decorations and flowers.

AMERICAN FROSTING

Makes 175 g/6 oz American frosting, sufficient to fill and ice the top and sides of a 20-cm/8-in sandwich cake.

1 egg white
175 g/6 oz icing sugar
1 tablespoon golden syrup
3 tablespoons water
pinch of salt
1 teaspoon lemon juice

Place all the ingredients in a basin over a saucepan of hot water and whisk until the icing stands in peaks. Remove from the heat and continue whisking until the mixture has cooled. Spread over the cake using a palette knife. This frosting must be used as soon as it is made.

ALMOND PASTE CHART FOR RICH FRUIT CAKES

	18 cm/7 in	20 cm/8 in	23 cm/9 in	25 cm/10 in	28 cm/11 in
	15 cm/6 in	18 cm/7 in	20 cm/8 in	23 cm/9 in	25 cm/10 in
Ground almonds	225 g/8 oz	350 g/12 oz	450 g/1 lb	575 g/1¼ lb	675 g/1½ lb
Icing sugar	125 g/4 oz	175 g/6 oz	225 g/8 oz	275 g/10 oz	350 g/12 oz
Caster sugar	125 g/4 oz	175 g/6 oz	225 g/8 oz	275 g/10 oz	350 g/12 oz
Lemon juice	1 teaspoon	1 teaspoon	2 teaspoons	2 teaspoons	3 teaspoons
Almond essence	few drops according to taste	few drops according to taste	few drops according to taste	few drops according to taste	few drops according to taste
Orange flower water	few drops according to taste	few drops according to taste	few drops according to taste	few drops according to taste	few drops according to taste
Eggs (beaten)	1	1	1	2	2-3

These quantities are sufficient to cover both the top and sides of the cake

Mix the ground almonds, icing and caster sugar. Add the remaining ingredients with sufficient egg to form a stiff, manageable paste. Knead until smooth.

Roll out one-third of the almond paste, large enough to cover the top of the cake. Brush the top of the cake with sieved apricot jam and place the almond paste on top. Trim level with the sides. Roll out the remaining paste into one long strip, the width of the sides, or two shorter strips, according to the size of the cake. Brush the sides with apricot jam and cover with the almond paste, sealing the edges with a palette knife. Leave in a cool dry place for 1-2 weeks.

ROYAL ICING CHART FOR RICH FRUIT CAKES

| | 18 cm/7 in | 20 cm/8 in | 23 cm/9 in | 25 cm/10 in | 28 cm/11 in |
	15 cm/6 in	18 cm/7 in	20 cm/8 in	23 cm/9 in	25 cm/10 in
Egg whites	2	3	4	4	4
Icing sugar (sieved)	450 g/1 lb	675 g/1½ lb	1 kg/2 lb	1 kg/2 lb	1 kg/2 lb
Glycerine	1 teaspoon	1½ teaspoons	2 teaspoons	2 teaspoons	2 teaspoons
Rosewater	few drops to taste	few drops to taste	few drops to taste	few drops to taste	few drops to taste

These quantities are sufficient to flat ice both the top and sides of the cake.

Place the egg whites in a bowl and whisk until just frothy. Gradually add the icing sugar, beating well until the icing is shiny and very white. It should be thin enough to spread but thick enough to hold its shape. Beat in the glycerine and rosewater. Keep icing in an airtight container for up to four weeks. Secure the cake to the board with a little icing and allow to set. Spread the icing on top of the cake with a palette knife, working out any air bubbles. Do not let any of the icing run down the sides. Hold a metal rule at an angle and draw it firmly across the top of the cake (see picture). Remove the icing from the rule immediately. Trim icing from the cake edges with a knife. Leave to harden before icing the sides.

Place the cake on a turntable or up-turned plate and spread icing on to the sides. If you are icing a square cake, ice opposite sides and allow to dry before icing the remaining sides. This will give good square corners. Holding a plastic scraper at an angle on the side of the cake, pull right round in one continuous movement, keeping your hand holding the scraper completely still (see picture). Leave to harden. Use fine glasspaper to sand off any rough edges. Repeat three or four times to finish.

PIPING ROYAL ICING DESIGNS

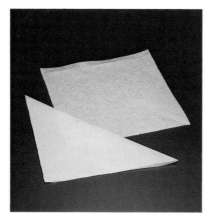

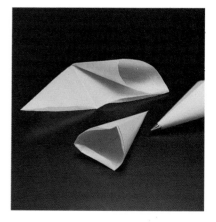

To make a piping bag, fold a 20-cm/8-in square of greaseproof paper in half to form a triangle.

With the wider edge of the triangle facing you, fold up the two outer corners to the central point at the top, making a crease along the fold lines.

Form into a cone shape, making sure the point is very firm. Staple or fold the ends of the bag to secure. Cut off the tip of the cone and insert the piping nozzle.

Designs using a star tube

Stars

Shells

Coils

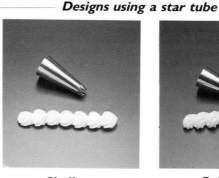

Writing

Designs using a plain writing nozzle

Straight lines

Beads

Continuous rope beading

Trellis

CHOCOLATE DECORATIONS

— *Chocolate leaves* —

Melt the chocolate in a basin over a saucepan of hot water. Wash and thoroughly dry the rose leaves. Brush the underside of the leaves with a layer of melted chocolate. Chill to harden. Carefully peel the leaves off the chocolate and chill until required.

— *Chocolate curls* —

Choose a chocolate that is not too brittle and a sharp knife with a straight blade.

Hold the blade of the knife at an angle to the block of chocolate and firmly shave a layer off to form a curl. Repeat until you have the required number of curls. Keep in the refrigerator until needed.

— *Chocolate shapes using cutters* —

Melt the chocolate in a basin over a saucepan of hot water. Spread out thinly onto waxed or greaseproof paper. Leave to set until just firm.

Using a ruler as a guide, cut the chocolate into a square with a sharp knife. Cut into squares which can be halved to form triangles. Keep in the refrigerator until needed.

Use cutters to cut out a variety of shapes. Keep the trimmings to melt down again. Take care not to handle the cut-out shapes too much as they will lose their gloss. Keep in the refrigerator until required.

CRYSTALLISED FLOWERS

Mix 15 g/½ oz gum arabic with 2 tablespoons rosewater and shake well in a screw-top jar. Leave for two hours. Make sure flowers are completely dry and unblemished.

Using a fine paintbrush, paint the flower petals all over with the gum arabic solution. Leave until the solution has been absorbed, then sprinkle all over with caster sugar.

Remove any surplus sugar and sprinkle again with sugar if required. Leave to dry and flowers will then become hard.

RUNOUTS

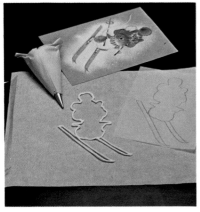  

Trace the chosen design onto waxed or greaseproof paper. Lay the paper on a flat board and secure. Lay a piece of waxed paper on top. Make up the royal icing and pipe along the outline using a greaseproof piping bag fitted with a writing nozzle. Allow to dry slightly.

With a slightly softer royal icing, flood the centre of the runout, using a cocktail stick to guide the icing into all the corners. Allow to harden. It is preferable to use icing without glycerine.

Carefully lift the runout off the paper. Paint the features using a food colouring and a fine paint-brush. Allow to dry before placing on the cake. Greeting cards are ideal for designing one's own runouts.

PIPED ROSES

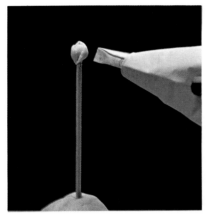

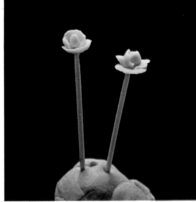

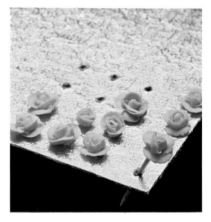

Make sure the royal icing is of a consistency that will keep its shape. Using a greaseproof piping bag fitted with a petal shape nozzle, pipe the centre of the rose around the point of a cocktail stick.

Twisting the cocktail stick between the thumb and the first finger, pipe the petals individually until the rose reaches the required size.

Push the bottom of the cocktail stick through a hole in a small piece of card to remove the flower. Allow to harden before using.

MOULDED FLOWERS

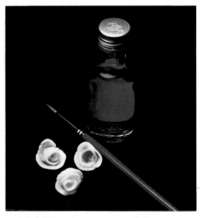

Press small pieces of fondant icing between your fingers which have been dipped in cornflour. Shape into individual petals. Roll the first petal to form the centre of the rose.

Mould each petal around the centre and build up into a rose. Cut off at the base of the rose if the petals have become too thick. Allow to harden.

Highlight the centre of the rose with food colouring using a fine paintbrush. Allow to dry before using.

Index